Southern California
Curiosities

Help Us Keep This Guide Up to Date

Every effort has been made by the authors and editors to make this guide as accurate and useful as possible. However, many things can change after a guide is published—establishments close, phone numbers change, hiking trails are rerouted, facilities come under new management, etc.

We would love to hear from you concerning your experiences with this guide and how you feel it could be made better and be kept up to date. While we may not be able to respond to all comments and suggestions, we'll take them to heart and we'll also make certain to share them with the authors. Please send your comments and suggestions to the following address:

The Globe Pequot Press
Reader Response/Editorial Department
P.O. Box 480
Guilford, CT 06437

Or you may e-mail us at:

editorial@GlobePequot.com

Thanks for your input, and happy travels!

Curiosities Series

Southern California
Curiosities

Quirky Characters, Roadside Oddities
& Other Offbeat Stuff

Saul Rubin

The
Globe
Pequot
Press

GUILFORD, CONNECTICUT

The information in this book was confirmed at press time.
We recommend, however, that you call establishments to
obtain current information before traveling.

Cover and interior photos by the author unless otherwise
noted.
Text design by Bill Brown
Layout by Debbie Nicolais
Maps by XNR Productions © The Globe Pequot Press
Cover photos by the author

ISSN 1547-8920
ISBN 0-7627-2724-1

Manufactured in the United States of America
First Edition/Second Printing

*For my wife, Bethany, whose love and support
make everything possible.*

ACKNOWLEDGMENTS

*I thank editor Mary Norris for finding me and
entrusting me with this project. I also thank so
many Southern Californians who shared their stories to make this book possible. Naomi—thanks for
help with printed documents.*

CENTRAL VALLEY,
DESERTS, AND
SEQUOIA NATIONAL PARK

CENTRAL
COAST

GREATER
LOS ANGELES

METROPOLITAN
LOS ANGELES

ORANGE COAST
AND SAN DIEGO
REGION

PALM SPRINGS ARE
AND
SOUTHERN DESER
REGION

Contents

Introduction
viii

Metropolitan Los Angeles
1

Greater Los Angeles
55

Orange Coast and San Diego Region
93

*Palm Springs Area and
Southern Desert Region*
139

*Central Valley, Deserts, and
Sequoia National Park*
179

Central Coast
219

Index
265

About the Author
269

INTRODUCTION

Southern California is a little like that high-maintenance girlfriend you find plenty to complain about but are destined to love anyway. There's trouble in paradise for sure, what with earthquakes, smog, and way too much tofu. But just when you're about to say, "So Cal honey, you're great, but I can't take another wildfire or freeway jam," you're reminded why you'll be forever hooked.

There's the obvious stuff, of course, like the gorgeous weather, the fabulous beaches, and the scenic mountains—and awesome produce or the fact that in Los Angeles you can get great Thai food, even at 2:00 A.M.

Then there are treasures that aren't as easy to spot. Like a virtual salad of vegetable and fruit festivals, including galas for the strawberry, carrot, avocado, and even the rumpled raisin. Or how about a cemetery that features art walks and a comedy show performed weekly in the most unlikely of settings: a Laundromat. Southern California boasts the most-photographed rest room in the world in an ultrakitschy inn along the Central Coast. There's also a town that prides itself on a unique civic treasure, an alley with walls stuck with wads of gum, decades old. Yuck, yes, but fascinating.

And the people. Oh, the people. Such as the guy in Fresno who constructed a wonderland of a home with exotic fruit trees, all 20 feet underground. Or the comedian in Bakersfield who struts around dressed like a chicken.

I never thought I'd speak so passionately about Southern California because I've always considered myself a Northern California guy. As such I was trained to have nothing but contempt for the state's southern half. I'm not alone. Interstate tensions run so high there are periodic rumblings of a divorce.

Californians must choose sides. It's north or south, Berkeley or UCLA, the Giants or the Dodgers, Silicon Valley or the Valley of Silicone Implants.

A funny thing happened to me in the course of writing this book. I warmed up to Southern California in a big way. Although I may not be able to show my face again in San Francisco, I've written this book to tell you about the many cultural riches I've discovered here. I gained something else, too: a new-found passion for Southern California, its offbeat culture, people, history, and even its ghosts. My own Eureka! moment.

As you flip through these pages, I hope you'll find it, too.

Griffith
Park

Studio
City

Laurel
Canyon

Hollywood

Los
Feliz

Silver
Lake

Echo
Park

East Lo
Angeles

West
Hollywood

Los Angeles

Santa Monica

Culver City

Marina
del Rey

Westchester

Inglewood

Watts

El Segundo

METROPOLITAN LOS ANGELES

Metropolitan Los Angeles

PINBALL WIZARD
Culver City

Boys have their heroes, and for Patrick Sheehy, it was the pinball repairman at the local bowling alley. While other teens idolized sports stars, Sheehy spent countless hours tagging along after the arcade repair guy as he tinkered with the inner workings of his beloved ball-and-bumper games.

Sheehy never outgrew his passion for pinball. As an adult he has acquired more than one hundred vintage arcade games and has opened a museum to share them with others. He enjoys watching first-time visitors stroll wide-eyed into his museum. "Their faces tell the whole story—they're like kids again," he says.

Sheehy displays about half his collection in his storefront museum, including the oldest, a 1952 wooden pinball bingo game called Key West. Most of his games date from the 1970s, the height of the pinball era, before they were Pac-Manned to death at the arcades by an onslaught of video games.

His museum doubles as a repair shop, where Sheehy is now the one tinkering with the guts of these vintage games. Pinball mechanics is "old school stuff," he says, with antiquated wiring and switches that control features such as bumpers, flashing lights, flippers, and spinning wheels.

Patrick Sheehy's got plenty of game, and it's all vintage.

Artwork and game themes reveal a bit of television history. Most are designed around old broadcast shows such as *Star Trek* and *The Six Million Dollar Man*. Others reflect cinema, including the game "The Wizard," linked to the film version of the Who's rock opera *Tommy* and featuring the likenesses of Roger Daltry and Ann-Margaret on the game board.

Bump your way over to the museum at 4350 Sepulveda Boulevard. Sheehy opens it Saturdays by appointment. Call (310) 391–2969.

A STOREFRONT OF WONDERS
Culver City

The most common misconception about the Museum of Jurassic Technology is that it's all about dinosaurs. It's not. Of course, just what the name really means is never explained by museum staff. A visit to this storefront collection of bizarre yet astonishing exhibits may not help, either. Visitors who venture inside its dark confines usually emerge more puzzled than when they arrived.

Part of the museum's mission is to create a sense of wonder. This is a museum that explores the idea of a museum. The journey includes some of the most peculiar items you'll likely find in a display case. One exhibit features a furry, hard protrusion that looks like a bony finger. Accompanying text describes the story of the unfortunate Mary Davis, who grew a horn from the back of her head. Another display features two dead mice laid neatly on a piece of toast, apparently representing a once-popular folk cure for the loss of bladder control.

Visitors can also ponder the miniature sculptures of Hagop Sandaldjian, including the figure of Disney's Goofy perched on top of a pinhead. Another display features detailed props and a text that explains theories of memory and forgetting by an obscure neurophysiologist named Geoffrey Sonnabend. It's an exhibit you're not likely to forget. The elfinlike mastermind behind this odd collection is David Wilson, fond of explaining his mission by offering up the museum's motto, *translatia natura*, which he says means "nature as metaphor." "If there is a thread that ties together the eclectic nature of the museum, it is that," he adds. If that helps explains things, use it.

Through the years Wilson has built a dedicated following among museum professionals and seekers of offbeat culture.

And recently he was honored with a MacArthur Fellowship worth $500,000, which should help secure the museum's financial future.

The Museum of Jurassic Technology is located at 9341 Venice Boulevard in Culver City. You can call ahead at (310) 836–6131 or visit a Web site at www.mjt.org.

AN EXHAUSTIVE COLLECTION
East Los Angeles

In an area of town where competition is stiff for auto-repair businesses, the El Pedorrero Muffler Shop has no problem standing out. Maybe it's the shop's bold blue-and-yellow checkerboard design that makes it look like a giant piece of pottery. Or the requisite "mufflero" man, fashioned from junk parts, who is stationed in front, along with a yellow-and-black car coated with dozens of chrome tailpipes jutting out at weird angles. The store's name, a slang term for flatulence, is a matter of curiosity, too, in this Spanish-speaking neighborhood.

The main draw here isn't mufflers but owner Bill London and his amazing collection of knickknacks. The husky and big-hearted London, a former military engineer, says he has more than a million items on display at his shop. Some are crammed into two auto bays, including an antique hot-dog stand, an expansive Chinese fan, duck decoys, a beat-up pressure cooker, antique clocks, decorative vases, and a row of old fire alarms. More stuff overflows on shelves and a desk in his office, dominated by a mounted deer head and an oversize Swiss army knife. London marvels at everything in his collection and hopes his visitors do, too. "See," he says, running his fingers along the etched glass of an Italian-made table, "art!"

The muffler man and oddball art collector, too.

London has also created his own folk works. One piece is a tiny sculpture of an antique car he formed by using an old harmonica, a screwdriver, beer-bottle caps, dice, and other found items.

Amid the eclectic displays, muffler work gets done. The museum is free, and London's pretty reasonable about his muffler work.

The El Pedorrero Muffler Shop is located at 4101 Whittier Boulevard and can be reached by calling (323) 264–6868.

The Semple Life
Echo Park

By the time she arrived in Los Angeles in 1918, Aimee Semple McPherson already possessed considerable skills as a Pentecostal evangelist who could whip a crowd into a religious frenzy. But it was in the shadow of a burgeoning Hollywood, with her dramatic preaching style and movie-star looks, that she really rose to prominence.

She made the Echo Park neighborhood of Los Angeles the spiritual center of her religious movement by building her magnificent Angelus Temple there in 1923. With its soaring dome made of crushed abalone shells and an auditorium that seated 5,000 of her fervent followers, the temple provided a perfect backdrop for her vaudevillelike sermons. She used movie props to illustrate her religious musings, once appearing dressed as a policewoman and warning her congregation to stop breaking God's laws.

She became the first woman to receive a radio license from the FCC when she launched her own station, KFSG, widening her reach and perfecting a broadcast preaching style that would be copied later by televangelists.

Her flair for the dramatic wasn't confined to the pulpit; it spilled over into her life, including a headline-grabbing disappearance in 1926 in which it was widely reported that she had drowned in the Pacific Ocean. Hundreds of her followers fruitlessly combed the beach for her body. More than a month later, McPherson turned up in Arizona and began telling a story about being kidnapped to the Mexican desert and her eventual escape. This twist, and subsequent investigation of her claims,

No one dozed off during her church services.

Photo: Courtesy Loyola Marymount University postcard collection.

were eaten up by the press and further elevated McPherson's celebrity status.

McPherson's Four Square Gospel denomination thrives at present as an international organization, and her church remains as well. In 2002 the Angelus Temple, at 1100 Glendale Boulevard, received a $7-million renovation that church followers say would make McPherson proud.

AFTERLIFE STYLES OF THE RICH AND FAMOUS
Hollywood

T yler and Brent Cassity raised eyebrows when they purchased a rundown cemetery here in 1998 and talked about
turning it into a cultural landmark.

True, it was no ordinary burial ground. The Hollywood
Memorial Park Cemetery was the resting place of many screen
legends, including Tyrone Power, Peter Lorre, Jayne Mansfield,
and Douglas Fairbanks Sr. *and* Jr. It was always worth a trip
here just to peek at Mel Blanc's gravestone, featuring his
famous sign-off THAT'S ALL FOLKS!

The memorial park, opened in 1899, was marketed as the
Cemetery of the Immortals in its heyday in the 1930s, when it
offered Hollywood celebrities the same red-carpet treatment in
death they were accustomed to in life.

In the 1990s the cemetery fell on hard times and the auction
block. That's when the Cassity brothers, St. Louis natives from
a family of undertakers, snatched it up and vowed to make it a
Hollywood star once again. They spent millions repairing the
crumbling mausoleums and fallen grave markers and eventually restored the sixty-two-acre site to its former glory.

Now named the Hollywood Forever Cemetery, it may be the
only burial ground in the country that features regular art
walks, jazz concerts, and film screenings. The cemetery is
famous for its annual Rudolph Valentino memorial tribute,
begun more than seventy-five years ago, when a mysterious
woman in black began visiting Valentino's crypt here at exactly
12:10 P.M. each August 23 to mark the date and time he died in
1926. The Valentino tribute now features an outdoor nighttime
screening of one of his films, shown on the mausoleum wall
that contains his crypt.

He's not kidding.

The Cassity brothers have added another twist to the funeral business: multimedia tributes of the newly departed. These digital productions are shown at funerals and are available for viewing in the cemetery's intimate six-seat theater, in special memorial kiosks, or by Internet downloads. So far the brothers have produced more than 15,000 of these digital biographies in a special studio on the cemetery lot, easily making them the hardest-working producers in Hollywood.

The Hollywood Forever Cemetery is located at 6000 Santa Monica Boulevard and can be reached at (323) 469–1181. An extensive Web site is found at www.forevernetwork.com, where you can view selected life stories of some of the cemetery's inhabitants.

Your Ticket to Hollywood
Hollywood

They don't serve alcohol here, but this Hollywood bar always draws a crowd. That's because it's the set of the famed television series *Cheers,* one of the featured exhibits at the Hollywood Entertainment Museum. No one is likely to shout your name in greeting as you walk into this neighborly joint, but you'll get a kick out of bellying up to the bar at Norm and Cliff's former watering hole. Museum visitors can also experience being transported to Captain Picard's command chair on the bridge of the *Star Trek* set or gawk at the office of Agent Fox Mulder of the hit TV series *The X-Files,* including trademark pencils stuck to overhead ceiling panels.

Though the museum has many fun exhibits, curator Jan-Christopher Horak says that its more serious intent is to give the public a behind-the-scenes look at how Hollywood creates its magic on film and television. "What we're trying to show is

The secret to great moviemaking: awesome props.

that it's real people working in crafts, and that movies are detailed, labor-intensive projects," he says. You can cower in fear as you walk through the gallery of monsters—real props from several horror films, including a menacing monkey from *Planet of the Apes* and a diabolical alien from *Independence Day*. Then go to a nearby exhibit area and make like a monster yourself and tower over a remarkable one-quarter-inch scale replica of Hollywood as it looked in the 1940s.

As a bonus feature, the museum inherited the Max Factor collection, exhibits that detail the career of the man credited with creating make-up for film and influencing everyday Americans to use it as well. Most peculiar is the Beauty Calibrator, metallic headgear that looks more like a torture device than something that Factor claimed in 1932 could be used to highlight points on a person's face that needed correction by make-up. "I think it was a publicity stunt," Horak admits. "I can't imagine a high-paid actress putting that pointy thing on her head."

The museum is located at 7021 Hollywood Boulevard. Call (323) 465–7900 for more information or visit the museum's Web site at www.hollywoodmuseum.com.

Look Who's Not Talking
Hollywood

In an age when movie-theater owners are proudly showcasing the latest high-tech gadgetry in sound and digital imagery, one theater delights in presenting film programs from the low-tech era of silent pictures. The Silent Movie Theatre is the last remaining silent-film theater in the country, a throwback to the days when screen actors overplayed their emotions and films were shown with live-music accompaniment.

The sad truth is that most films from the silent era are gone, either from neglect or deterioration. The debut in 1927 of the legendary first talkie, *The Jazz Singer,* signaled the end of silent films. By the 1940s most theater owners wanted the latest in sound pictures for their audiences, except for John and Dorothy Hampton.

HOLLYWOOD HYPE

*J*ust nine metal letters perched on a small mountain summit, the HOLLYWOOD sign is one of the world's more photographed and easily recognized landmarks. And in true Hollywood fashion, the sign's history is full of dramatic plot twists.

Originally it read HOLLYWOODLAND, erected in 1923 by real-estate developers to promote a housing subdivision in nearby Beachwood Canyon. It was a grand promotion on par with a studio production, featuring 45-foot-tall letters visible for miles. Quickly the sign became a symbol not of land for sale but of the moviemaking industry. To prove the point, an actress despondent over her film career clambered up to the letter H in 1932 and jumped off, becoming the sign's first suicide.

The sign suffered through a noir period during the 1940s, the victim of vandalism and neglect, and by decade's end the sign dropped its last four letters and was sold to the city of Los Angeles. The sign was declared a city cultural landmark in 1973, but during the 1970s and 80s it didn't get any respect from pranksters, who altered its appearance to suit their whims. It read OLLYWOOD during the Iran-Contra hearings, HOLLYWEED after the state passed a new marijuana law, and, somehow, Go NAVY when Navy played a football game at the Rose Bowl.

Presently the sign is watched over by a special trust and is maintained by funds raised through the sale of licensed merchandise. Though most tourists are satisfied with snapping pictures of the famous landmark from a distance, its closeness and accessibility by trails lures some to strive for a more intimate encounter. Hiking to the sign is illegal, however, and a sophisticated surveillance system records lawbreakers on special video monitors stationed at a nearby Griffith Park ranger station—not the most ideal way to launch a film career in Hollywood.

The silent treatment.

This Oklahoma couple arrived in Los Angeles with the goal of opening up a silent-movie theater, and they did it in 1942, screening Cecil B. DeMille's epic *The King of Kings*. John Hampton single-handedly restored many silent films during the next few decades, helping to preserve historic treasures that might have otherwise been lost, as most studios had given up on them.

The Hamptons closed their theater in the 1970s, but a family friend, Laurence Austin, reopened it in 1991. Unfortunately, Austin was gunned down in the theater lobby in 1997 in a murder-for-hire crime in which Austin's business partner sought to collect his inheritance. Eventually, another silent-film buff, Charlie Lustman, came to the theater's rescue and reopened it in 1999 with the screening of Charlie Chaplin's *Modern Times,* the last silent feature film ever made.

Now the theater has regular screenings on weekends and is available for special bookings. For more information call (323) 655–2520. The theater is located at 611 North Fairfax Avenue.

M M M . . . . B I G D O N U T
I n g l e w o o d

Here's a donut so massive it might even satiate Homer Simpson's craving. Then again, maybe not. But this concrete, plain cake colossus is a vision all right—22 feet high and seemingly poised to crush the drive-thru donut shop it rests upon.

The spherical cake suspended over Randy's Donuts is the most famous of four remaining in the Los Angeles area, which at one time had many of the oversize treats, according to Randy's owner Ron Weintraub. It has been featured in books, magazines, rock videos, and movies. "Everything but legitimate stage," Weintraub says.

Located near a major freeway and the airport, the monster donut was erected in 1953 and designed by Robert Graham, known in Los Angeles for having created the headless and naked athletic figures erected at the Los Angeles Memorial Coliseum in honor of the 1984 Olympic Games.

Asked if the giant donut helps business, Weintraub quickly replied, "Oh yeah." Most passersby crane their head upward to get a glance. Once they straighten out their necks, they head to the shop to satisfy a sudden craving for a donut.

A big donut, yes, but you should see the size of the oven that cooked it.

To a more sophisticated audience, the giant donut is a prime example of programmatic architecture—buildings that look like what they sell. To the rest of us, it just looks like one big donut.

You can't miss Randy's Donuts at 805 West Manchester Boulevard, or call (310) 645–4707.

THIS RECORD LABEL IS FOR THE
BIRDS . . . AND OTHER CREATURES
Laurel Canyon

Skip Haynes toiled for years as a professional musician and songwriter, but his career took off only after he sang a duet with a parrot.

His singing partner, Carla, is a yellow-topped Amazon parrot fond of squawking, somewhat musically, "Zippety-do-dah, I'm a green chicken."

Haynes mixed Carla's "singing" with his own lyrics to create a country ballad called, what else, "I'm a Green Chicken."

The single was released worldwide and appears on *Bird Beat,* the third album by the Laurel Canyon Animal Company, a label Haynes created with partner and neighbor Dana Walden. It's probably the first recording label in the United States devoted entirely to animal music.

"It started as a goof," says Haynes. "We just said, 'Jeez, we can pick any animal and do a song about it.'"

The label's first two releases were *Ugly Dogs Need More Love,* and *Cat-a-Tonic.* Now there are plans for several more albums featuring other nonhumans including dolphins, horses, and gorillas.

Though most of the label's songs involve people singing about animals, the occasional furry-throated voice, like Carla's, gets a turn at the mike. Carla performed like a pro, completing her track in just two takes. "We didn't manipulate her voice at all. Just used a little reverb," says Haynes.

He and Walden were so impressed that they went to their friend, Dean Kay, a board member of the American Society of

Composers, Authors, and Publishers, and asked if he could arrange to get Carla registered as a songwriter.

"After he stopped laughing, he actually took our request to the board," Haynes said. But the board had bad news for the bird: no social security number, no songwriting credit.

Guess she'll just have to settle for a cracker.

You can order a CD from Laurel Canyon Animal Co. by calling (800) 233–2880.

S HELVES OF S PELLS
L o s   A n g e l e s

M artin Mayer has brought sorcery into the age of the mega-store with an improbable warehouse-size outlet devoted to magic potions. Mayer says that his Indio Products Company is the world's largest manufacturer and distributor of esoteric items, and one visit to his store, situated on a commercial street southwest of downtown, confirms his claim. Shelves are jammed floor to ceiling with a spellbinding array of magical potions, oils, lotions, candles, soaps, and assorted enchanting scents. All of Mayer's products are designed to bring good fortune into someone's life, be it luck with money, love, job, business, or even legal matters. He even produces something called Make Opposing Lawyer Stupid Oil, which you might want to lather on before heading into court.

Think someone's out to get you? Try the Go Away Evil cologne, which tells users to "surround yourself with a protective scent to block spells." If that doesn't do it, try Go Away Evil floor wash. Yes, it's a floor wash *and* a magic potion, available in either eight- or sixteen-ounce jugs.

Mayer says that almost all of his products fall under the category of white magic, designed to bring good luck to users, as opposed to black magic, which is geared to doing others harm.

One of the many ways to change your luck.

"Everything here has a meaning, and the people here believe in it," Mayer says as he watches shoppers load up carts with bulk-size containers of his magic stuff. Mayer says that followers of the Caribbean-based religion of Santeria use some of his products, whereas most are used by true believers looking for a bit of superstitious luck. Everything's brewed up at his manufacturing plants in nearby Long Beach, then sold by catalog or direct to the public in his Los Angeles store.

You'd think with more than 7,000 products surrounding him all geared to promoting good luck, some of it would rub off on Mayer. But no. "Every time I go to Vegas, I lose," he sighs.

The Indio Products store is located at 236 West Manchester Avenue and can be reached at (323) 778–2233. A Web site is at www.indioproducts.com.

HANGING OUT WITH A FAST CROWD
Los Angeles

One of Los Angeles' core fundamentals is its car-based lifestyle, what with its myriad freeways and pedestrian-unfriendly streets. That's why you have to wonder what Cheryl Anker was thinking when she opened her unique business aimed at showing off Los Angeles to out-of-towners on foot. Not walking, by the way, but *running*.

Her Off 'n Running Tours offers visitors a chance to see Los Angeles at a jogger's pace. For $50 the marathon coach and race director will lace up her running shoes and take runners through the streets of Los Angeles on some of her favorite training routes, including through the beach cities and Beverly Hills. "When people come to L.A., they think there is nowhere to run, or they are afraid to go outside to run. But once they do it, they're amazed at how beautiful parts of Los Angeles are," she says.

Just don't expect running commentary as you jog along with Anker. And don't try to set any speed records, either. "I tell people it's not a race. The longer I've been doing this business, the slower the running gets," she says with a laugh.

For more information call (310) 246–1418.

LITTLE GIFT SHOP OF HORRORS
Los Angeles

For the Los Angeles County Coroner's Office, death makes for a lively business.

Since 1993, the coroner's office has been operating a one-of-a-kind gift shop that offers an impressive array of souvenirs built around the department's morbid business of processing bodies. Among the more popular items are beach towels that feature a chalk body outline, authentic toe-tag key chains, and T-shirts emblazoned with the coroner's seal on the front pocket and a coroner's body logo on back.

A conversation starter at the beach.

Called Skeletons in the Closet, the gift shop began modestly enough in a tiny closet at the coroner's downtown office, but it's no longer a bare-bones operation. The store ships more than 30,000 mail-order catalogs worldwide each year and now has a major marketing presence on the Internet, where sales have been brisk. Its popularity has grown mostly by word of mouth. "I can't do traditional advertising," admits James Hazlett, a coroner-department marketing analyst. "Some people might think it was in bad taste."

Store proceeds benefit the coroner's successful anti-drunk-driving program aimed at area youth. For such a worthy cause, shop operators keep churning out new merchandise, such as body-shaped Post-it pads, undertaker boxer shorts, "Sherlock Bones" tote bags, and a mouse pad with a white body outline that reads: "We're dying for your business." As the store's motto says, this is a gift shop for those with "dubious distinctive taste."

It all makes going to the Coroner's office, at 1104 North Mission Road, something to look forward to. Call (323) 343–0760 for more information or visit the shop's Web site at lacstores.co.la.ca.us/coroner/signpost.htm.

THE REALLY BRIGHT LIGHTS OF L.A.
Los Angeles

The fact that certain gases, especially neon, could be electrified to create a luminescent splendor visible for miles was discovered in Paris in 1898. It didn't take long before savvy American entrepreneurs envisioned neon's marketing potential. America's neon era was launched in Los Angeles in 1923, when car-seller Earle C. Anthony lit up two orange-and-blue signs over his dealership and created a sensation. By the 1930s

Someone's bright idea for a museum.
Photo: Larry Lytle.

America's landscape was dotted with these "ribbons of living flame," many of them infused with splendid artistry of color and movement.

The neon era eventually faded, but by century's end enjoyed rekindled interest thanks in part to institutions such as the Museum of Neon Art in Los Angeles, the only museum of its kind in America. Founded in 1981 by artist Lili Lakich, the museum's mission is to preserve vintage neon signs as well as to showcase works from the burgeoning neon-art movement.

The museum, housed on the ground floor of an apartment building in downtown, rotates items from its permanent collection and also produces several temporary shows each year that feature works by a new generation of neon artists.

Though advertisers favor neon because it burns the brightest, artists utilize an array of other noble gases with subtler tones, including xenon, argon, krypton, and helium. Some of these works are more abstract and thus not easily understood, but one thing's for sure: No one can say they can't see them.

The museum always leaves a light on at 501 West Olympic Boulevard. It also sponsors nighttime bus tours for viewing historic neon signs throughout the area. For more information call (213) 489–9918 or visit the museum's Web site at www.neonmona.org.

STRANGE ENCOUNTERS OF THE AIRPORT KIND
Los Angeles

The Theme Building at the heart of Los Angeles International Airport, with its parabolic arches and spiderlike form, has always looked like an oversize prop from a B-grade sci-fi flick. Dedicated in 1961, the building was designed with a space-age look. In 1996 a whimsically futuristic lounge and restaurant was added to the building's top floor to complete the picture.

Arrive at night at the Encounter Lounge and Restaurant and you'll be greeted by a light show of magenta, electric blue, and white. Eerie lounge music and sound tracks piped into the elevator set the mood on the ride up. The folks at Walt Disney Imagineering designed the restaurant's decor, and reviewers have characterized it as either Jetsonlike or something that Austin Powers might favor for his shag pad. There's the crater-shaped bar, moonstone countertops with colored lava lamps, amoeba-shaped ceiling fixtures, and a wall that resembles a lunar landscape. To add to the fun, the restaurant staff wears

A PRESERVATION EFFORT TAKES OFF

*E*very day hundreds of jets soar out over the ocean under the watchful eye of the Los Angeles International Airport. Beneath this noisy flight path, the airport monitors another kind of flyer—a pint-size flutterer known as the El Segundo Blue Butterfly.

Although only about the size of a quarter, the El Segundo Blue has thrown its weight around in preservation circles. In 1976 it became the first insect on the federal endangered-species list. The butterfly's numbers had dwindled because its prime food source, the coast buckwheat, was overrun by development and squeezed out by the invading ice plant.

Concern over jet noises forced the airport to purchase a 300-acre site west of the airport and clear out a neighborhood, eventually making way for a butterfly preserve on the coastal dunes favored by the El Segundo Blue. The butterfly has so much community support for it that plans for an 18-hole golf course on part of its habitat were scrapped out of fear it would hurt its chance for survival.

Preservation efforts have done so well that the butterfly population now numbers 50,000, proving that it can flourish under the steady roar of overhead jets. Of course, the other local habitat favored by the El Segundo Blue is in another undesirable neighborhood: the grounds of a nearby oil refinery.

appropriate space-age costumes, and the bar's soda guns emit laser lights and special sound effects.

The menu here offers something else unusual for an airport eatery: fine dining and an excellent wine list. The bar is known for its specialty martinis.

After refreshments, take the elevator up to the rooftop observation deck and see what air travel is really like as you get a panoramic view of planes zooming in and out of the airport. A long flight delay was never so enjoyable. Jet over to the Encounter Lounge and Restaurant at LAX at 209 World Way. For more information call (310) 215–5151.

HE'S GOT THE WORLD ON A STRING
Los Angeles

Bob Baker was hooked when he saw his first puppet show at age six. He drove his parents crazy until they got him what he wanted: his own puppet set and stage. When he was eight, he turned pro, performing with his puppets at a birthday party and earning $15. "This was in the Depression, and that was good money," Baker recalls. So he stuck with it.

He later designed puppet animations for department-store windows, performed puppetry for the film industry, and forged a lucrative career making puppets for Disney. In 1960, hoping to showcase his puppetry skills to earn more television appearances, he opened a theater just west of downtown Los Angeles. "What it did instead was open the door for more theater," Baker says with a laugh.

Baker says his Marionette Theater is the oldest working puppet theater in the United States. With a repertoire of fifteen

Bob Baker likes to string people along.

shows, the theater performs elaborately staged and marvelously entertaining shows that enthrall kids and adults. The theater's winter *Nutcracker* performances are so popular that sold-out shows are extended past Christmas into January.

The theater's carpeted performance area is rimmed by metallic chairs, upon which adults perch. Kids sit on the floor and interact with the puppets, operated by black-clad puppet masters, all trained by Baker. All the puppets are made in the theater's back workshop.

After each show kids are served ice cream, cookies, and juice in a party room decorated with giant lollipops and pink chairs. "Kids relate to puppets more than they relate to cartoons," Baker says. After more than forty-three years of puppet theater, Baker has no intention of slowing down. He plans to launch a show geared to an audience at the other end of the age spectrum: seniors.

Bob Baker's Marionette Theater is located at 1345 West First Street. Reserve tickets by calling (213) 250–9995.

THE PITS OF HISTORY
Los Angeles

In the heart of a city where forward-looking inhabitants are always scouting the next big thing, the folks at the Rancho La Brea Tar Pits buck the trend by focusing deep into the city's past. That's way back, as in 40,000 years or so.

The La Brea site is of one of the richest fossil finds in the world, representing one of the most diverse collections of ice-age plants and animals ever unearthed. And you can thank the area's natural underground muck for making it all happen.

THE OTHER WRIGLEY FIELD

With its ivy-covered walls and storied history, Wrigley Field in Chicago is certainly a legendary field of dreams. But even some baseball purists may be surprised to learn that at one time there was another Wrigley Field with ivy-covered walls where professional baseball was played—in south-central Los Angeles.

Wrigley Field in Los Angeles was built in 1925 and designed as a 20,000-seat replica of its Chicago counterpart as the home field for William Wrigley Jr.'s Los Angeles Angels, who played in the Pacific Coast League. Though made to look like the real Wrigley, the Los Angeles version had California touches, including a Mission-style red roof and white facade. The Los Angeles Wrigley also added stadium lights in 1931, decades before Wrigley Field in Chicago would follow suit.

The stadium was a crowd pleaser and attractive enough to be in the movies, serving as the backdrop for a series of Hollywood baseball films, including Damn Yankees. But its ivy-coated walls were a nightmare for one of the team's stars, Lou "Mad Russian" Novikoff. It was rumored that Novikoff's bouts of poor fielding in left field were due to his fear of vines, which he denied, saying his problems stemmed from a crooked field.

Though the Angels were at the Triple-A level and used by Wrigley as a farm team for his Chicago Cubs, the team provided major-league excitement for local baseball fans who had to wait until the arrival of the Dodgers and the American League Angels for major-league franchises.

The Pacific League Angels left town in 1957, and the last strike for the Wrigley replica came in 1966, when it was torn down to make way for a community center.

"I've fallen, and I can't get up!"

Thousands of years ago, underground and naturally occurring crude oil bubbled to the surface to create thin sheets of sticky asphalt that trapped, and then magnificently preserved, hapless numbers of passing animals. Caught in the sticky asphalt were saber-toothed cats, giant ground sloths, mammoths, bears, and an untold number of other small plants, birds, and animals. About four million fossils have been recovered from the site so far, offering perfect documentation of what life was like in Los Angeles 10,000 to 40,000 years ago.

Fossil recovery is still under way, and during an eight-week period each summer, visitors can watch as paleontologists and volunteers dig for more in the site's Pit 91.

After watching the workers burrow through the 28-foot-square pit, visitors can head to the nearby George C. Page Museum of La Brea Discoveries to examine some of the fossil finds already recovered, including an amazing wall of dire wolf skulls, one of the most common finds at the excavation site. Visitors can also peer at museum workers as they sort through hundreds of fossil bones in a glassed-in laboratory.

The museum, with a large bubbling pond of muck in front, is located at 5801 Wilshire Boulevard. Call (323) 934–7243 for more information or visit the museum's Web site, www.tarpits .org, to find out when the annual summer dig will be held.

A PRAYER FOR FIDO AND FOR EVERY OTHER CREATURE, TOO
Los Angeles

They come by the hundreds each year—barking, bleating, and screeching, on wings, four legs, and sometimes slithering—to receive what their owners feel is rightfully theirs: a blessing. Equal parts spectacle and ritual, the annual Blessing of the Animals in downtown Los Angeles is a long-standing tradition that beckons creatures from all parts of Southern California.

The procession of animals usually features standard pet fare such as dogs and cats but also includes chickens, turtles, llamas, iguanas, hamsters, and, one year, a bejeweled bug. Many come wearing elaborate outfits or in wildly decorated cages. They parade along the city's historic Olvera Street and are sprinkled with holy water by the leader of the Roman Catholic Church's Los Angeles Archdiocese.

The unique ceremony is mostly a Latin tradition and is celebrated by other area churches twice a year—during the Feast of St. Francis of Assisi in the fall and on Holy Saturday, the day before Easter. But the one downtown (held during Easter) is the granddaddy of them all, and some families have made it a tradition dating back generations.

In a much newer tradition, the B'nai Tikvah congregation in nearby Westchester began its own Celebration of the Animals in 1996, believed to be the first time anywhere that a synagogue has sponsored such an event. B'nai Tikvah's animal blessing takes place in the fall during the yearly Torah reading of the story of Noah's ark.

EXHIBITS TO DIE FOR
Los Angeles

James Healy is dead serious when he says his unique collection of artifacts is really an appreciation of life. True, he's named it the Museum of Death. And yes, the exhibits are decidedly morbid, including a gallery of coroner photographs, assorted execution devices, mortician's equipment, and—a recent acquisition from Paris—a severed head.

"I think that it shocks people, but it's a good shock," Healy says. "Seeing all these artifacts of death in one place reminds people how precious life is," he says, and visitors to his museum often leave with a more positive outlook on things.

Then again, some visitors have simply fainted away at the displays, in fact, twenty-three of them during a recent six-month period. "I had a big football player pass out in front of one of the coffins," Healy says, adding that he never knows what might make a person lose it.

Healy admits to a fascination with death, and he decided to share it with the public in 1995 by opening a museum in a fashionable shopping area of San Diego. Five years later he moved his collection to Hollywood and added significant pieces, including Jayne Mansfield's stuffed Chihuahua, Liberace's dead cat, and artifacts from the Heaven's Gate cult. His Heaven's Gate extensive collection includes some of the outfits members were wearing when they committed suicide in 1997 in hopes of a rendezvous with a space ship that was supposedly trailing the comet Hale-Bopp. Healy set up the Heaven's Gate artifacts as a diorama.

What Healy hasn't figured out is how to exhibit a two-headed turtle, one of the specimens he has left over from the time he began a collection for a freak farm.

Healy is hoping to breathe new life into the Museum of Death in a new location. To check on its status, call (323) 255–3319.

A CEMENT RIVER RUNS THROUGH IT
Los Angeles

Leave it to Los Angeles, one of the most developed urban areas of the world, to have a river made of concrete. Los Angeles is not as bad as Cleveland, of course, where a river once caught fire, but the L.A. River's limpid flow and concrete-lined banks have made it the butt of many jokes. Even worse, many locals don't even know it exists.

The Los Angeles River runs for 51 miles from western San Fernando Valley, passes north to south through downtown Los Angeles, and empties out near the *Queen Mary* in Long Beach. Centuries ago it was a vibrant riparian ecosystem that supported countless trees, plants, birds, and animals. But it proved

Grab a cement boat and take a ride.

too wild and flood-prone for development-minded civic leaders, and in 1938 a project began to pave it over, relegating the river to the role of flood-control channel.

At present, if the river's running at all, it looks more like a trickling drainage pipe than a pulsating waterway. Its graffiti-marked levees further mar the river's appeal as a recreational destination. The river's unusual setting, however, has made it a favorite with movie producers, who have used it countless times as the backdrop for gritty urban dramas.

Hope is on the horizon for the river, although revival efforts have been fighting an upstream battle for years. Various volunteer groups have created small greenbelt areas along sections of the river, adding basic recreational features such as walking trails, bikeways, and park space. And a newly formed City Council committee is looking into ways to promote the river's renaissance, adding further optimism for the future of the concrete river.

RECREATION GALORE. . . AND A LONG-AGO CURSE
Los Feliz

With more than 4,100 acres of lush hills and glens, Los Angeles' Griffith Park is the largest urban park in the country. More than ten million visitors a year enjoy its hiking trails, golf courses, and other recreational and cultural offerings, including the Griffith Observatory and Greek Theater. But lurking beneath the park's verdant scenery lies a not-so-pretty story about how the sizable expanse of land came to be donated to the city in the first place.

The land that is now Griffith Park was part of a much larger tract known as Rancho Los Feliz. The last Feliz to own the property, Don Antonio Feliz, died of smallpox in 1863. The bachelor bypassed his sister and niece in his will and instead gave the land to Don Antonio Coronel, who suspiciously helped Feliz draw up the will when Feliz was on his deathbed. Believing she had been cheated out of her inheritance, Feliz's niece, Patranilla, unleashed a curse upon Coronel and the land by declaring that the "vengeance of hell shall fall upon this place."

Calamities followed sure enough. For unknown reasons Coronel unloaded the land to his lawyer, who was subsequently shot and killed. The ranch was then sold to Leon "Lucky" Baldwin, but his fortunate name didn't help with the running of the place. Cattle died, crops fell victim to fires and pests, and a dairy on the property turned into a disaster. For unknown reasons ostriches being raised there were prone to stampeding at night.

Baldwin eventually sold the property to Griffith J. Griffith. With ranch hands reporting ghost sightings on the land, Griffith preferred to visit only during the day. Eventually he felt compelled to donate the land to the city for use as a park in 1896. Apparently this benevolent gesture pleased restless spirits because the curse ended once the city acquired the property.

W HO   Y OU   G ONNA   C ALL?   T RY   T HIS   G UY
M a r i n a   d e l   R e y

W hen Larry Montz saw his first ghost as a ten-year-old while visiting his aunt's house, he wasn't particularly scared. He just marveled at the way the ghost, a woman in a gray dress, was able to appear and disappear and walk through walls.

"Ghosts are nothing to be afraid of," Montz says, and he enjoys studying them. He's a modern ghost buster, employing a sophisticated array of monitoring equipment and a stable of talented clairvoyants to solve mysterious ghost sightings around the world.

"Any place people have lived and died has the potential for a haunting," Montz says. "If that thought gives you the shivers," he adds, "don't worry." A common misconception about ghosts, perpetuated by media and religion, is that they're demonic. In reality they're mostly just confused, he explains, or have unresolved issues that keep them earthbound.

Most people who call Montz are nonetheless scared and looking for answers. And Montz can help, along with the investigators and psychics he has assembled at his International Society for Paranormal Research. He can tell clients not only if a place is haunted but by whom and why.

If you think you're psychic and might want to join Montz's team, you can take a test on-line at the group's Web site, www.ispr.net. If you're worried about a ghost, give them a call at (323) 644–8866.

A HOLIDAY TREE THAT DOESN'T NEED WATERING
Santa Monica

When Anthony Schmitt was asked to develop a Christmas decoration for the Edgemar building in 1995, he knew it was a challenge. After all, the angular complex of arty stores with a trendy restaurant and hip coffee shop was designed by whimsical architecture-wonder-boy Frank Gehry and was already something of an art piece in itself.

As Schmitt mused upon supermarket shopping carts, he had a revelation, and though his idea seemed unconventional at the time, it has now become a Santa Monica holiday tradition: a towering, 30-foot Christmas tree constructed entirely of shopping carts. The unique tree, decorated with large metallic ornaments and topped with a capricious Santa doll, dominates the complex's courtyard each December.

"I wanted to do something that provoked some commentary," says Schmitt, and he has clearly succeeded. Passersby do double takes, whereas locals don't feel the Christmas season has arrived until the shopping cart tree is erected. Tourists pose at its base for a unique photo op; others sit at tables in the complex courtyard sipping coffee and contemplating the significance of a metallic tree. Is it a commentary on the commercialization of Christmas, or just another sign that

Try getting these carts back in the corral.

things are different in this part of the country? Or is it a shrine to the homeless, who are often seen pushing shopping carts around town?

"Sometimes people lose sight of the meaning of Christmas, as if it's just about the gifts," Schmitt says. "It's kind of like renewing that sense of innocence and wonder as opposed to getting trapped into what it has become."

Schmitt, an artist who used to design window displays for Barneys New York, rents the carts each year and has a preference for ones without a bottom compartment because they appear more "branchlike," he says. Then it's just a matter of mounting the carts to a base and stacking them up in a tapering fashion. "At night, from the street, it looks just like a tree," Schmitt says proudly.

To see for yourself, you can visit the shopping-cart tree at the Edgemar complex every December at 2427–29 Main Street.

NIGHT OF THE DOLPHINS
Santa Monica

Southern Californians are used to the occasional sighting of dolphins frolicking in the ocean. But a vision that catches many by surprise is the spectacle of a neon-blue dolphin cavorting through the air while trailing a bicycle rolling along the streets. Yes, dolphins are intelligent, capable creatures, but they have their limits. And romping through traffic is one of them. The pedaling porpoise is actually an illusion created by Jeff Frymer.

Frymer was motivated by the eclectic artworks he spotted at Nevada's Burning Man Festival a few years ago. He designed the dolphin animation using special electroluminescent wire

Even Flipper couldn't ride a bike. Photo: Duncan Stewart.

that lights up when charged with current. What looks like a dolphin rising out of the water and then flopping back into the ocean is actually several dolphin images that light up in sequence to create the simulated movement. The animation panel is attached to a 6-by-6-foot mesh screen and towed behind Frymer's bike, using a makeshift trailer he crafted from pieces of aluminum mounted on wheels.

Frymer says the magical display took more than 200 hours to build. He takes it out at night and rides along the coastal bike path or sometimes through the streets. Friends have requested that he bring it to birthday parties and other special events.

"All the money and time I spent on it comes back to me in the amount of appreciation I get from people," he says. "When people see dolphins, even though it's a wire animation, they cheer and yell and say, 'Wow, that's really cool!'"

A FEAST FOR THE EYES
Silver Lake

Clare Crespo's great adventure with food began with a Jell-O recipe book her father gave her when she was a kid. "I was crazy about that book. I tortured my family with it," she says. It was Jell-O mold after mold, ever more elaborate.

"I've always been a real goofball in the kitchen," she says. Food is her palette, a way to make sustenance more palatable. As an adult she's found a way to make a living by playing with her food. She's published a popular cookbook, *The Secret Life of Food,* offering forty-six whimsical recipes such as Spaghetti with Eyeballs, a pasta dish with stuffed olives that look like eyes. The book includes directions for making an edible aquarium with blueberry gelatin for water, fruit cocktail for aquarium gravel, and candy fish suspended in the mold.

Crespo has knit plates of food such as ham and eggs and a grilled-cheese sandwich and has exhibited them in galleries around town. She's also available for challenging food commissions, having once been hired to do a family portrait in mashed potatoes. "One employer hired me to do a birthday cake. He said it had to have a circus theme, feed 250 people, and blow

There's something fishy about this aquarium.
Photo: Clare Crespo.

everyone's mind," she recalled. She answered the challenge by creating a life-size cake of fire-breathing Siamese twins with red-whip licorice arteries. It blew everyone's mind all right, and was pretty tasty, too.

Crespo came to California to get a master's degree in animation and then worked as a producer of music videos. Now her creative efforts are geared to culinary arts.

"My kitchen is kind of my studio," she says. It has lots of Jell-O and candy around, raw material for her imagination. "I love to cook regular stuff, but it's more fun to put a twist on it. But if I'm by myself, I won't try and make a peanut-butter sandwich look like a monster," she admits.

If you'd like some of her recipes, visit her Web site at www.yummyfun.com.

CRUSADER OF THE LOST ARK
Silver Lake

Antonia F. Futterer was a real Indiana Jones, without a bullwhip but equally adventurous. In fact, it has been rumored that he was the inspiration behind the movie character.

When Futterer's prayers for recovery from severe appendicitis attacks were answered, he became a firm believer in the Bible, eventually setting off on a quest for the Golden Ark of the Covenant in 1926. By then he had made several trips to holy lands and had begun a collection of artifacts from exotic locations, including Syria, Jordan, Egypt, Cyprus, and Palestine. He brought his treasures back to Los Angeles and founded a Bible school and museum devoted to his collection.

Futterer died in 1951, but his collection lives on in the Holyland Exhibition, five display rooms in a large home in a residential area. Overseeing the collection is volunteer Betty

Are you my mummy?

Shepard, who came to the house to study the Bible and became a full-time resident in 1978.

In the Damascus section visitors can marvel at a game table made with 10,000 pieces of inlaid mother-of-pearl and wood from fourteen different fruit trees. In the archaeology room is a wall with miniature glass paintings that depict biblical highlights. Other items in the eclectic collection include three ears of now-extinct Egyptian corn, precious stones, pottery shards, and a chunk of salt said to be piece of Lot's wife. An Egyptian exhibit features a 2,600-year-old mummy case given to Futterer by Egypt after the 1933 Chicago World's Fair.

After each guided tour Shepard treats visitors to a grape drink, some Mandel (almond) bread, and apricot fruit leather, imported from Damascus.

The Holyland Exhibition is at 2215 Lake View Avenue. Tours are available seven days a week anytime, but you must call ahead for a reservation: (323) 664–3162.

CLEANING UP THEIR ACTS
Silver Lake

When Christy Murphy asks comics if they're interested in doing a few minutes of stand-up comedy in a Laundromat, they're apt to think she's joking. After all, she's a comedian, too.

But Murphy's dead serious, at least about her weekly comedy show, held in a working Laundromat before a small but dedicated audience of regulars. Then there's the not-so-dedicated group of spectators who just show up to do their laundry, not knowing that while their underwear and towels were getting a wash, they'd be subjected to a comedy spectacle as well.

Each Wednesday evening in the cavernous laundry, as dozens of washers and dryers tumble and churn, Murphy sets up a mike just outside a bathroom door and begins hosting a ninety-minute set of several stand-up acts. The obvious question, of course, is why. "I guess it's the novelty aspect of it. It's so awful you have to do it," she laughs. "We've gotten some pretty amazing comedians to come in here and do their comedy in front of a bathroom door next to the dryers."

Some like the low-key venue because they can try out new material without fear of having some studio executive in the audience, in case the new stuff bombs. Murphy said she likes

Where dirty jokes get clean.

the idea of the captive audience—even if they don't like the jokes, they're not going anywhere, at least until their laundry dries.

All Washed Up is held each Wednesday at 8:00 P.M. at Lucy's Laundromat, 2134 Sunset Boulevard.

Just Lounging Around
Silver Lake

L ounge acts have always walked a fine line between kitsch and hipness. That's probably why they're so easily parodied—consider Bill Murray's schmaltzy act years ago on *Saturday Night Live.* In the late 1990s the meter tilted toward coolness for lounge music during a revival period fueled partly by the popular film *Swingers.*

Through the ups and downs, there has been one constant in the Los Angeles lounge scene: Marty and Elayne at the Dresden Room. In this quintessential lounge bar and restaurant, with big leather booths and perfect martinis, Marty and Elayne have performed their special blend of music for more than twenty years.

As the audience huddles in the dimly lit space or nibbles on appetizers such as garlic-cheese toast or mozzarella marinara, the duo swings their way through an eclectic play list that includes American pop tunes and bebop jazz. Elayne works away on the organ and flute, while Marty keeps pace on the drums. Both sing and sometimes scat their way through musical fare ranging from standards such as "I've Got You under My Skin" and "Fever" to jazz classics such as Charlie Parker's "Anthropology."

"If you have stuff you'd like to hear, say it—we'll play it," Marty says, keeping up a constant banter with the engaged crowd throughout the evening. If they find out it's your birthday, they'll launch one of the most fast-paced birthday songs on the planet.

If all the hot music makes you work up an appetite, slide over to the restaurant on the other side of the frosted Art Deco glass. There you'll find high-backed pristine-white booths, spiraling gold Venetian chandeliers, and a menu that includes steaks and pasta, of course.

Marty and Elayne perform Monday through Saturday from 9:00 P.M. to 1:15 A.M. at the Dresden Room, located at 1760 North Vermont Avenue. For more information call (323) 665–4294.

A SALAD THAT DELIVERS
Studio City

When Ed LaDou opened his Italian restaurant, he expected it would become popular for its gourmet pizzas. But another item on the menu made his cafe famous: a salad rumored to send overdue pregnant women into labor.

The rumors started in 1993, LaDou recalls, when a pregnant woman well past her due date stopped by and ordered the cafe's romaine-and-watercress salad. The next day she went into labor, believing that the salad had triggered her delivery. So she sent an overdue pregnant friend to the restaurant, and soon after, another baby was on its way. As word spread, a legend was born: LaDou's salad, and more importantly, its potent balsamic-vinegar dressing, could induce labor.

At first LaDou loved the publicity. Media descended from all parts of the globe to report on the magic dish, and business picked up. LaDou was mailing the dressing to frustrated expectant mothers. But then he soured on his special vinaigrette. "I thought, if I'm going to be famous, let it be for something I've created and not by accident," he moaned.

He tried to divert attention from the labor-inducing myth, but overdue pregnant women can be a relentless force. They just kept coming and ordering it up. Though some obstetricians were skeptical, others perpetuated the salad myth and gave it a medical endorsement by advising overdue patients to go to the cafe and have it for lunch. Some even conceded that the dressing might contain ingredients that could trigger uterine contractions.

Now LaDou has made peace with his special salad and welcomes about fifty pregnant women a week to his restaurant. He's even making plans to market the dressing in stores as the "maternity salad."

"We've got something; maybe it's not infallible, but if a woman is close to the edge and needs that gentle nudge, this just might be just enough of a nudge to help her along," LaDou says.

If you'd like to sample the salad, stop by the Caioti Pizza Café at 4346 Tujunga Avenue in Studio City (818) 761–3588. And please, someone in the party make Ed happy by ordering a pizza, too.

An In-Spiring Landmark
Watts

When Simon Rodia moved onto a tiny, wedge-shaped plot of land in Watts in 1921, he had in mind "to do something big." For the next thirty-three years, using simple tools, the construction worker and Italian immigrant toiled nights and weekends to create a series of fanciful spires that would eventually be hailed as a folk-art masterpiece and a tribute to one man's determination and quirky artistic vision.

Rodia eschewed a drill, welding torch, and scaffolding. Instead, he worked by hand, first assembling steel-reinforced rods and wire mesh, then coating them with cement and encrusting the concrete with a mosaic of bottle shards, seashells, rocks, and pieces of ceramic tile. Historians point out that Rodia preferred the green glass of 7-Up bottles and the blue from Milk of Magnesia containers.

Convinced his work was finished in 1954, he gave the property to a neighbor and left for Northern California, never to return. Some people believed that what he left behind held up as a cultural landmark equal to the Eiffel Tower, but others questioned whether it would hold up at all. Los Angeles building inspectors tried to demolish the structures as being unsafe soon after Rodia left, but community supporters organized a highly publicized stress test in 1959 to show that the towers were secure.

Rodia's work is now known as the Watts Towers. Maintaining them through the years has been problematic, as financial support has shifted among local, state, and federal governments. The towers were closed to the public for seven years for a major $1.9-million restoration following damage from the 1994 Northridge earthquake and were reopened with a gala celebration in 2001.

The Towers are located at 1727 East 107th Street. Tours can be arranged by calling (213) 847–4646. The Watts Towers Art Center, a city-operated facility next door, offers art classes and special exhibitions and can be reached by calling (213) 485–1795.

ONE-CENT HISTORICAL TREASURES
Westchester

The glorious age of the picture postcard was launched at the end of the nineteenth century in the United States when Congress passed a law allowing privately printed cards. Before you could say "Wish you were here," a vacationer's standby sentiment to those left behind, there were postcards from

A postcard view of history.

Photo: Courtesy Loyola Marymount University postcard collection.

everywhere. They depicted locales from the grand to the mundane, from landmark buildings to obscure meatpacking plants.

Vintage postcards are now prized not so much for their scribbled greetings but for what's on the reverse side: a slice of history revealing everything from what places long gone once looked like to social attitudes, fashion, politics, and sometimes important news of the day.

That's why Loyola Marymount University has a historian's treasure in what is a most unusual research archive: more than one million postcards stored in forty metal cabinets at the school's Von der Ahe Library. The collection was donated to the university in 1967 by Werner von Boltenstern, a German-born postcard collector who settled in Los Angeles in 1950.

One card shows a picture of the California Alligator Farm, a now-defunct tourist attraction. Dozens of World War II–era postcards reflect much about American life during this arduous period. Some are works of art, such as one from the St. Louis World's Fair of 1904. It shows the Palace of Education, and when held to the light, it illuminates the pavilion's windows and boat lanterns in brilliant reds and yellows.

The collection is available for viewing by appointment by calling (310) 338–3048.

A MAN OF A THOUSAND FACES
West Hollywood

If you ask Sig Shonholtz for the time, he should be able to tell you. After all, he owns more than 1,000 wristwatches, and they're all ticking away in perfect working order. These are not mere timekeepers, however, but finely crafted antique and contemporary showpieces designed as much for their form as function.

Shonholtz is a third-generation jeweler and watchmaker, a tradition that began when his grandfather opened a jewelry store in Philadelphia in 1898 and then relocated to Los Angeles in 1918. Shonholtz says he literally grew up in the store sorting precious stones and spending countless hours watching the store's craftsmen create beautiful custom-made jewelry pieces and watches. As a teenager Shonholtz studied with an old watchmaker and learned the craft for himself, knowing then he would carry on the family tradition of fine watchmaking.

As Shonholtz became expert at antique-watch restoration, he knew it was time to open his own business. He established the Second Time Around Watch Company in 1976, believing that there was a market in men eager to make a fashion statement on their wrist. "Men don't have a lot of ways to distinguish

Watch out for this guy.

themselves in the workplace with accessories," he says, "except for wearing a distinctive belt buckle, ring, or wristwatch. I tapped into that very early."

Now he's riding a wave of popularity in antique watches and catering to customers worldwide, some who stop by his shop in an antique emporium and others who buy directly from his Internet site. Though most restored watches can fetch a few hundred dollars, others, he explains, sell for a few million to serious collectors, which points toward a bright future in the antique-watch market.

Second Time Around is located in the Antiquarius Center at 8840 Beverly Boulevard and can be reached by calling (310) 271–6615. Visit the Web site at www.secondtimearound watchco.com.

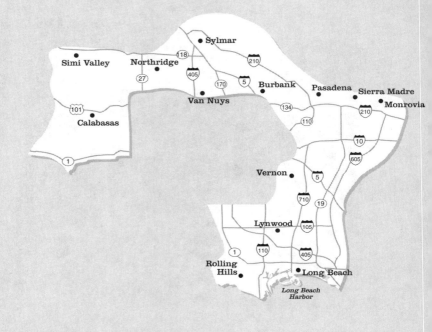

GREATER LOS ANGELES

Greater Los Angeles

A HOP BACK IN TIME
Burbank

Southern Californians spend so much time in their cars they end up doing loads of activities while driving such as applying make-up or reading the paper. Eating while driving is another favorite pastime. A safer and more relaxing alternative is eating while parked at Burbank's historic Bob's Big Boy restaurant. Bob's offers throwback 1950s-style-carhop service on weekends, reviving a slice of Americana tied to an era of poodle skirts and the greaser look.

Burbank's restaurant, built in 1949, is the oldest surviving Big Boy in America, an architectural monument featuring the chain's pompadour-coiffed mascot, a 70-foot-tall neon sign, and a massive horizontal roof reminiscent of the popular 1950s design known as "coffee shop modern." The look belongs to architect Wayne McAllister, who helped build early Las Vegas and defined nightclub chic of 1950s Los Angeles when he constructed several popular lounges.

Waitresses don't wear roller skates because of liability concerns on carhop nights, one concession to modern times. But they come to the driver's side window to take your order and then deliver it on trays that attach to car doors.

The menu hasn't changed much here in half a century, but regulars say that's a good thing. On Friday nights the restaurant parking lot is a hangout for owners of classic cars, so diners get a free antique-car show along with their burger and shake.

You can hop on over to Bob's Big Boy at 4211 Riverside Drive. Carhop service is Saturday and Sunday from 5:00 to 10:00 P.M.

PERPETUAL PETS
Calabasas

Some pets get treats. Others get mausoleums.

From parakeets to famous horses and dogs, scores of beloved pets earn a classy final tribute at the Los Angeles Pet Memorial Park, the oldest pet cemetery in Southern California. Los Angeles veterinarian Dr. Eugene C. Jones opened the ten-acre site in 1928, and ever since it has been the burial ground of choice for esteemed pets.

More than 40,000 animals are buried here, including some who had famous companions, such as Charlie Chaplin's cat, Humphrey Bogart's dog, and the adored pets of Harry James, Gloria Swanson, Mae West, and Steven Spielberg. Animals that were stars in their own right are also memorialized at the park, including Topper, Hopalong Cassidy's horse; Spot, the dog from the *Little Rascals;* and Petey, the black-eyed dog from *Our Gang.*

The grounds feature hundreds of grave markers that express an outpouring of love for mourned four-legged friends, including a monument dedicated to Tawny, a lion who died in 1940. Jones donated the cemetery to the Los Angeles Society for the Prevention of Cruelty in Animals in 1973, but when it appeared that the group might sell it to developers, it was bought by a nonprofit organization known as SOPHIE, Save Our Pets' History in Eternity. The group helped get a state law passed in 1986 that protects the cemetery from outside development, ensuring that pets such as Kabar, Rudolph Valentino's dog, will never be disturbed during their eternal rest. You can pay your respects at 5068 North Old Scandia Lane or phone (818) 591–7037 for more information.

PAWS ON PARADE
Long Beach

On a recent sunny Easter afternoon, Joyce Shimizu relaxed on a grassy spot with her twelve-year-old golden retriever Murphy. They were about to take a stroll, which seemed normal enough, except Joyce and her pooch were outfitted in matching hand-made bunny suits adorned with colorful pompoms, which attracted some attention on this day. But not as much as you'd think, as they were surrounded by dozens of other dogs in a startling array of outlandish outfits. There were greyhounds in bonnets, terriers sporting beanies, shepherds toting colorful Easter baskets, and a poodle wearing a sweater, to name a few. They were set to march in a newly minted holiday tradition in Long Beach: The Haute Dog Easter Parade.

The uncanny canine procession began in 2001 as a charity event organized by Justin Rudd, who, among other things, helps train contestants for beauty pageants. By the looks of this parade, these pups are as well behaved as any Miss America contestant. Sporting tuxedos, rabbit ears, and fancy hats, they stroll confidently along Second Street in Belmont Shore, where several hundred people howl with delight as each costumed canine struts by. Periodically the dogs pause like celebrities on the red carpet as camera-toting spectators snap away at the wild spectacle.

They say that owners start looking
like their pets.

Though some pooches stick to the Easter theme, others express themselves in more outrageous fashions. There are hounds dressed like chickens, and some that look like rock stars. This is one parade that clearly is going to the dogs, but in a good way.

The event is usually held the Saturday before Easter at 2:30 P.M. and runs along Second Street between Park and Nieto Avenues. For more information visit the Web site at www.hautedogs.org.

A NARROW VIEW OF HOME LIFE
Long Beach

There are times when J. T. Tyler convinces himself that he doesn't live in America's skinniest house. "When you're sitting in a room, you can psych yourself out that you're in a regular house," he says. But the three-story English Tudor–style stucco structure is anything but ordinary. It has been recognized by *Ripley's Believe It or Not* and the *Guinness Book of World Records* as being the country's thinnest home. At 10 feet wide, it's about the width of the driveway next to it. The branches of the spreading magnolia tree out front have more breadth. The house has only 860 square feet of living space.

When Tyler bought the tiny residence in 2002, he was aware of its architectural uniqueness. The real draw may have been the lack of choice in the Long Beach area. "The market is kind of thin for real estate. This definitely stood out in terms of character," said Tyler, a salesman. He gets more than the occasional visitor dropping by for a peek, and depending on his mood, he'll sometimes offer free tours.

The home's unique construction dates to a challenge issued in 1931 to the original owner, Nelson Rummond, who acquired

You can be as big as this house and still be thin.

the narrow lot as payment for a debt. A friend bet him that he couldn't build a home on such constricted turf, and Rummond met the challenge by hiring unemployed craftsmen to develop the unique house. It was completed a year later, creating a sensation. Since then, thousands of visitors have stopped by, including Walt Disney, who must have thrilled at seeing the whimsical, almost fairyland living quarters.

Despite its limited space, Tyler says he's never felt confined because of the home's comfortable layout, which includes a living room and kitchen on the first floor, and a bedroom, bath, and office space upstairs. The home, located at 708 Gladys Avenue, is listed as a historical landmark by the city of Long Beach.

A GRAVE FASCINATION
Long Beach

Whenever Clarence Williams saw hearses as a kid, he was so enthralled by their black sleekness and brocade curtains that he believed they were station wagons for the rich. When he got older, he realized what they were for, but he never lost his appreciation for their beauty.

He's no ghoulish loner, however; he's a member of the Phantom Coaches Hearse Club in Long Beach, more than one hundred everyday folks who adore cruising around in the one vehicle most of us would have to be caught dead to ride in.

Williams, of Santa Ana, owns a 1973 Oldsmobile hearse that barely fits into his garage and prompts wide-eyed stares from neighbors. "It's not a good daily driver," he admits. "You can't whip into a U-turn, and going through a drive-thru restaurant is out of the question."

OLD GLORIOUS

One day while motoring down the 405 Freeway, Thomas "Ski" Demski confronted his destiny in the form of a giant U.S. flag magnificently fluttering outside an auto dealership He returned to his Long Beach house and erected a 132-foot flagpole in front. He aptly called it The Pole, to designate what it was and also to pay tribute to his Polish heritage. And then he began buying immense American flags to fly on it.

His flags got bigger and bigger until he became the owner of the world's largest flag, a 255-by-505-foot banner that earned him a place in the Guinness Book of World Records. Demski's Super Flag debuted at the Washington Monument in 1992 and has made numerous appearances at high-profile events such as the Super Bowl and, in 1996, at the Hoover Dam as the Olympic-torch rally went by.

Demski said he never made much money from toting around his colossal flags for display, although longtime friend Jim Alexander says Demski made a nice living selling bumper stickers. Displaying his flags was his passion, even on his own body. When a tattoo artist noticed that a heart-surgery scar on his chest would make a great flagpole, Demski added flag tattoos that covered his torso.

Some people didn't share his enthusiasm, however, and there were occasional complaints about the size of his flagpole and the excessive noise his immense banners made while flapping in the wind. But Demski survived any legal threats to his displays.

Demski staged his own funeral in 2000 so that his friends would know just the kind of send-off he wanted. He imagined everyone eating sandwiches and gathering in his garage to admire his dermal display of Old Glory as he lay shirtless in a mirrored coffin, and that's how it was at his real funeral two years later, as Demski was remembered for his Super Flag and larger-than-life patriotism. Demski's flagpole still stands proudly at 402 Lime Avenue.

Ski Demski loved his colossal flags.
Photo: Thomas L. Demski Trust.

Other drawbacks include difficulty in finding a parking space and the abysmal gas mileage, about 7 miles to the gallon. And because most hearses aren't built for passenger comfort, there's usually no radio or air conditioning, either.

Hearse Club members organize monthly outings, usually to car shows, parks, and, of course, the occasional cemetery. They love caravanning to Vegas. During Christmas season they deck their hearses in lights and drive around town for a macabre holiday tribute.

Naturally, club members are much in demand at Halloween for special events and parties. Two years ago the club set a world record with a procession of eighty-six hearses that opened up Knott's Scary Farm, a proud milestone for the club.

Some members engage in a little black humor, like one who drives around with a fake arm dangling from the back and another with a vanity plate that reads Comin4U. The group's newsletter is called *The Epitaph*. Perhaps the group's motto says it all: "We put the fun back in funeral!" You can contact them by phoning (435) 603–0282 or visiting the group's Web site at www.phantomcoaches.org.

SHIP OF GHOULS
Long Beach

With its Art Deco styling and overall elegance, the *Queen Mary* was certainly a stylish transport when it sailed during the period of 1936 through 1967. At present some people believe that some of ship's crew are still onboard, albeit in spirit form. That might explain the odd rumblings and apparitions reported since the liner docked for good in Long Beach and became a popular tourist site and floating hotel.

Did you hear that creaking sound? Photo: Courtesy of *Queen Mary.*

Forty-nine deaths were reported onboard during the ship's history—and so forty-nine reasons to have restless spirits rattling its decks. Stories include those of the crushed crewman, the lady in blue, the phantom piano player, the little girl who wants to play, and the woman in white. The crushed crewman, for instance, was an 18-year-old deckhand violently killed in the ship's engine room during a routine watertight door drill in 1966. Since then some visitors have reported seeing a bearded young man in overalls suddenly appear near the doorway where the accident took place—doorway number 13, of course. Others have reported spotting mysterious watery footprints near the first-class swimming pool, even though the pool has been drained. One guide noticed a woman in a vintage bathing suit preparing to dive into the pool. When the guide called for security, she suddenly vanished.

Operators of the vessel haven't shied away from promoting these sightings, knowing that potential phantom encounters are a draw to some visitors. The ship hosts a weekend paranormal convention and regular tours devoted to the liner's spirited hot spots. For more information visit the ship's Web site at www.queenmary.com or call (562) 435–3511. The ship is located at the south end of the 710 Freeway in Long Beach.

How Ice Hockey Would Be Played If All the Ice Melted
Lynwood

Steve Herbert calls himself a "water nut." So it's not surprising that when he took up hockey, he ended up playing it in the water—actually underwater—whacking at a weighted puck with a 1-foot-long stick at the bottom of a pool and trying to shoot and score while frantically holding his breath.

That's the sport of underwater hockey, and though it's not exactly ready for prime time, it does have a few followers in the United States. Herbert leads the Los Angeles Underwater Hockey Club, one of a few in the country where an estimated 2,000 players partake in the sport.

"The neat thing about it is that it's three dimensional. You can dive down on top of people," Herbert says. Players don snorkel, fins, and protective headgear and slash at the three-pound puck with a short stick, trying to push it into 9-foot-long goals at either end of a pool. There are six players to a team. Slap shots travel about 3 feet underwater, so working with teammates is essential to success. "Timing and passing is everything," Herbert says.

Underwater hockey is bigger elsewhere—in countries such as England and Australia—but there actually is a governing body, here—the Underwater Society of America. World championships are held every two years, although the sport has limitations when it comes to gaining fans, because viewers have to be seated underwater to catch the action live.

One major difference between underwater and ice hockey is that there's no contact allowed in the underwater version. Too bad. It would be interesting to observe hockey fights in the decidedly slow-motion environment of underwater.

The Los Angeles club scrimmages two days a week at the Lynwood Natatorium. For more information you can contact them at (310) 314–4652.

CATCHING UP WITH BASEBALL'S LESSER-KNOWN MEMORABILIA
Monrovia

Terry Canon's oddball collection of baseball artifacts isn't destined for the sport's official Hall of Fame in Cooperstown. That's just fine with Canon, who believes he's honoring baseball players and folklore that may be overlooked in official circles.

His eccentric compilation, known as the Baseball Reliquary, has been called the Left Coast Hall of Fame. What else could you say about a collection that features such memorabilia as a fossilized, half-eaten hot dog presumably once munched by legendary slugger Babe Ruth, or a half-smoked stogie also attributed to Ruth?

"It's ridiculous for us to try and compete with the Baseball Hall of Fame," Canon concedes. "We look for artifacts that tell interesting stories."

Who knew a half-eaten hot dog could make history?

Photo: Larry Goren.

Canon began seriously collecting in the 1980s and organized the Reliquary with some friends in 1998. The group organizes exhibits at local venues, such as one centering on food and baseball. This display includes the preserved potato that was once disguised as a baseball and thrown in a minor-league game in one of baseball's classic stunts. There's also the Walter O'Malley tortilla, which bears a remarkable likeness to the former Los Angeles Dodgers owner. Supposedly, discovery of the tortilla by a Chavez Ravine resident in 1959 convinced her to peacefully leave the neighborhood and make way for the construction of Dodger Stadium. As Canon says, "Every artifact tells a story."

The Reliquary sponsors an annual dinner at which it elects new members to its Shrine of the Eternals. Recent inductees include Mark "The Bird" Fidrych, a Detroit Tigers pitcher in the 1970s famous for talking to the baseball before he hurled it, and Bill Veeck Jr., the iconic owner of the St. Louis Browns, known for challenging baseball's establishment and staging outrageous promotions. He once sent the pint-size Eddie Gaedel up to the plate in a 1951 game so that he could earn a walk, one of baseball's more mythic at-bats. Although the Baseball Hall of Fame has Gaedel's jersey, the Baseball Reliquary boasts a unique artifact commemorating this stunt—Gaedel's jock strap.

For more information about the Reliquary, visit its Web site at www.baseballreliquary.org.

VIEWING EARTHQUAKE DAMAGE IN A NEW LIGHT
Northridge

When an earthquake opened a crack in her bathroom wall, Marjorie Sievers marveled at how a vine grew into the newly opened space. When a major earthquake in 1994 devas-

A Truly California Bear

In 1994 a large black bear wandered into a Monrovia backyard. That wasn't unusual, for residents here were accustomed to crossing paths with wildlife, including bears, from the nearby foothills of Angeles National Forest. Most animals stroll into town in search of food or water, but this bear had other plans.

His goal was a relaxing dip in a backyard hot tub, all caught on tape by the homeowner. The tape showed the bear merrily splashing around and, at one point, leaning back in the tub with a contented look. After his frolic the bear was captured and scheduled for euthanasia. Luckily, a widespread airing of the home video rallied the public to his support, and the bear was pardoned.

Dubbed Samson, the bear was shipped to a new home at the Orange County Zoo where he enjoyed such amenities as a 12-foot waterfall and a bear-size swimming pool. Crowds flocked to see the famous hot-tubbing bear who adored avocados. He even inadvertently planted two avocado trees when he accidentally stepped on some pits within his enclosure.

Samson was euthanized in 2001 at age twenty-seven after suffering kidney failure. But his memory endures in the town of Monrovia, where a statue of Samson stands at the city's Canyon Park nature center, dedicated to the "understanding and respect for wildlife and their habitat." Maybe all we need to do to bridge the gap between people and animals is to throw one big hot-tub party.

tated the school where she got her art degree, Cal State University, Northridge, she saw something amid the rubble that others didn't. "In the contorted and bent structures were shapes and forms that reflected elements of beauty," Sievers says.

As the university was rebuilt, Sievers quietly collected bits of debris, planning an art project with it. In 2003 her unusual work was dedicated, making it one of the most oddly themed sculpture gardens in the country. Named after a late former Northridge faculty member, the Lauretta Wasserstein Earthquake Garden features twisted rebars, fallen columns, buckled concrete, and mangled railings, all presented as sculptures.

Created by Sievers and landscape architect Paul Lewis, the garden also has reddish concentric circles emanating from a center of green glass shards to represent seismic waves. Two benches in the garden were built from part of a parking structure wall that had collapsed during the quake.

Eventually, as the garden is planned, the grasses and vegetation planted around these unique sculptures will grow and obscure the works as nature takes over the art work. University officials praise their new garden, saying it celebrates the school's resiliency during its recovery efforts. The sculpture garden is located just off the Lindley Avenue and Nordhoff Street entrance to the campus.

Hare Today, Thousands Tomorrow
Pasadena

Everyone knows how quickly rabbits reproduce, but can the same be said about toy bunnies? Apparently yes, if you're Steve Lubanski and Candace Frazee. When Frazee and Lubanski were married, he wore a rabbit costume and bunny-hopped down the aisle. The wedding cake? Carrot, of course.

One bunny in this house led to thousands of others.
Photo: The Bunny Museum.

The couple went hopping mad when Steve gave Candace a
white plush bunny on Valentine's Day in 1992. The following
Easter, she returned the favor, giving Steve a white porcelain
rabbit. Before you could say, "What's up, Doc?" their Pasadena
home was overtaken by rabbit-themed collectibles as they began
a daily exchange of bunny gifts.

They're not shy about their bunny fetish, having turned
their home into a museum, open by appointment. Visitors can
gawk at the bunny-shaped toilet seat, bunny-themed planters,
and an Elvis-shaped water pitcher with a rabbit head that says,
"Elvis Parsley." Six live bunnies also roam the house.

The bunny-happy couple hopped right into the *Guinness
Book of World Records* in 1999, setting the mark with the
most rabbit-themed collectibles at 8,437. Frazee says the num-

ber is actually quite higher, but the Guinness people count pairs and sets as only one item. So bunny earrings are just one item, and the same for the salt-and-pepper bunny set; even a set of twelve bunny forks counted as only one.

Nevertheless, that slight hasn't stopped Steve and Candace from making every day a hoppy one, as they say on their outgoing phone message.

Hop on over to The Bunny Museum at 1933 Jefferson Drive. Call (626) 798–8848 or visit www.thebunnymuseum.com for more information.

A Snap That Crackles and Pops Eardrums
Pasadena

Yes, almost everyone can snap his or her fingers, but only one person in the world can do it as loudly as Bob Hatch. He suspected he might have a special talent when, as a kid, he walked through school halls snapping his fingers and angry teachers scolded him for making too much noise.

As an adult, he noticed people putting their hands over their ears whenever he got to snapping, so he contacted the folks at *Guinness Book of World Records* for recognition. He's now listed as the world's loudest finger snapper with a record 110 decibels, which he says is the equivalent of a dragster roaring down the strip or the noise level of a rock concert.

Hatch, who is left-handed, uses his right hand to produce the mighty snapping, employing the middle finger and thumb. But it's not just the fingers that do the trick. "It's a technique where my whole arm, neck, and head get into it," he says. When word got out of his piercing snapping, Hatch was interviewed for the local newspaper and appeared as a guest on

THE SCENIC RAILWAY THAT COULD

Decades before Disneyland, the prime tourist attraction in Southern California was a white-knuckle journey up the side of a mountain that took riders through dozens of hairpin turns over steep terrain along a narrow track that seemed to climb to the heavens. The Mount Lowe Scenic Railway was a tourist's thrill ride along 7 miles that snaked its way along the mountain areas above Pasadena. In a land devoted to private-automobile culture, the railway afforded Southern California a rare first in public transportation, as it is recognized as the world's first electric-powered mountain railway.

The Scenic Railway opened in 1893, the dream of inventor and scientist Thaddeus Sobieski Lowe and engineer David Macpherson. Lowe had already made a name for himself by promoting a balloon corps for use in the Civil War, creating the world's first military air force. Long-fascinated with celestial observations, Lowe often climbed into the mountains near Pasadena when he arrived there in 1887, and he soon launched construction of the cable and rail line that would be known as the Railway to the Clouds.

The railway operated until 1937, transporting up to 1,500 passengers daily. At the end of their journey at the base of Mount Lowe, riders encountered a minicity that featured a casino, an observatory, a zoo, a hotel, dining facilities, and gardens. As this period was known as the Great Hiking Era, there were plenty of trails available to explore. For kicks at night there was the world's largest searchlight beaming down upon the cityscape below, a beam visible as far away as Catalina Island.

Unfortunately, as the tracks climbed higher and higher, Lowe lost more and more money, eventually losing control of the railway. Disasters of biblical proportions, including fires, floods, landslides, and a massive wind storm eventually destroyed most of the rail line and the attractions at the base of Mount Lowe. The site is now listed on the National Register of Historic Places, although present-day visitors can get their thrills there the old-fashioned way: by exploring the area on foot.

A snap-happy family. Photo: Bob Hatch.

several radio programs, including one show where he was asked to snap to the theme song from the classic television series *The Addams Family.*

Hatch's record may not stand for long, as his own two sons are challenging him. It turns out that thunderous finger-snapping runs in the family. Hatch's grandfather was also known for his earsplitting snaps, and his sons have exhibited the same flair. The only one seemingly not impressed with all the deafening snapping in the Hatch household is Hatch's wife. "She just kind of walks away shaking her head," he says.

PEAK ENERGY

Majestic Mount Baldy, the 10,064-foot mountain in the San Gabriels, has been revered by countless religious and spiritual-minded folks for having immense karmic energy. One group of flying-saucer enthusiasts has worshiped the mountain's special powers for several decades ever since a London cabby-turned-spiritual-leader identified Baldy as one of the world's holiest mountains.

Enlightenment came to George King in 1955 when he heard voices from outer space calling him through "cosmic transmissions." The interplanetary connection led King to found a religion of UFO believers known as the Aetherius Society. He said voices from outer space instructed him to visit nineteen different mountains and channel specialized energy on their peaks to help make the world a better place.

King came to Mount Baldy in 1959 and eventually, in nearby Hollywood, built a temple that now serves as the group's headquarters. The group believes that an extraterrestrial craft, known as Satellite No. 3, has been orbiting the Earth since contact was first made with King, all the while radiating cosmic and solar energy that's there for all to receive.

Although King died in 1997, the Aetherius Society remains active in Los Angeles and organizes regular treks to the top of Baldy to keep the good vibes flowing for us all.

For more information on the Aetherius Society, call (800) 800–1354 or visit the group's Web site at www.aetherius.org.

A REVOLUTIONARY TOY
Pasadena

Ed Headrick believed in flying saucers, at least the plastic kind. When the Wham-O Company, based in San Gabriel, California, asked him to design a new toy using leftover plastic, Headrick decided to update a simple disc toy, which was not very popular at the time, by adding design features such as a black painted ring, a gold-foil label, and a depiction of the Olympic rings. He patented the device in 1967 as a flying saucer but marketed it as the Frisbee.

The Frisbee soared in popularity, partly because Headrick turned players into club members, forming the International Frisbee Association in 1967 and organizing the first World Frisbee Championships at the Rose Bowl in Pasadena, close to Headrick's own birthplace in South Pasadena.

When interest in the Frisbee Association waned, Headrick spun off the new idea of disc golf. There are eighteen holes, and players try for the lowest scores, but that's where the comparison to real golf ends. Players of disc golf flip flying discs into elevated baskets attached to poles. Headrick designed the world's first disc golf course at Pasadena's Oak Grove Park in 1975. Like the Frisbee, disc golf has proven to be anything but a fad. There are now more than 1,000 disc golf courses in the United States and an estimated three million regular players, according to the sport's governing body, the Disc Golf Association.

Headrick died in 2002 but got his wish, which was to keep on spinning. He asked that his ashes become part of several memorial flying discs, which were given out to family and friends.

A THORN IN THE ROSE PARADE'S SIDE
Pasadena

Each New Year's Day, millions of people turn their attention to Pasadena to watch one of the world's most famous processions, the Tournament of Roses Parade. Another Pasadena parade, with less of a following and a decidedly different sensibility, has also become a local tradition.

The Doo Dah Parade is the Rose Parade's zany alter ego. Locals started it in 1978 to goof on the Rose Parade. The Doo Dah is the Rose Parade without manners and polished style. It features screwball acts such as the Barbecue and Hibachi Grill Team, who cook hot dogs as they march and then shoot them into the crowd, using a custom Dog-A-Pault. Throwing food at spectators, in fact, is an honored Doo Dah tradition.

Past marchers include the Briefs Brigade, who stride along sporting white boxer shorts, and the Sierra Pacific Fly Fishers, who twirl fishing lines while keeping rhythm to the music. One year a group strutted the parade route outfitted as a human burrito, with marchers dressed as beans, lettuce, and sour cream paced behind a large tortilla.

For a brief period the Doo Dah Parade flirted with becoming part of the establishment it so wanted to mock when organizers agreed to live-television coverage. But the experience took away some of the event's charm and spontaneity, so they chucked the coverage. You'll just have to watch it live as you duck the flying food. To find out parade dates, call (626) 440–7379.

VERY SWEET ONIONS

In the rush to tell California's gold history, one story is often overlooked. It not only involves gold, but also onions, and it took place much farther south and a few years earlier than John Marshall's Eureka! moment at Sutter's Mill near Sacramento.

As the story goes, and it has several variations, herdsman Francisco Lopez awoke from an afternoon siesta in March of 1842 after napping under a large oak tree. He had dreamt of floating in a pool of liquid gold. Stirring, he remembered that his wife had asked him to bring home some wild onions, so he began picking some growing near the tree. He got his onions, and a lot more, because he noticed gold flakes hanging from the roots of the onions.

Tests confirmed that the flakes were indeed gold and that his dream of floating in wealth was suddenly a reality. Lopez's discovery was six years before Marshall's, and it set off a minirush of prospectors into the area that is now known as Placerita Canyon. The recovery rate was slow, possibly as little as a few dollars of gold a day, but the area was mined for the next few years and made some people moderately wealthy, although no one can say for sure if one of them was Lopez. Though Marshall is the man most people credit with discovering gold in California, it was really Lopez who unearthed the state's first significant gold strike. A plaque was dedicated in 1935 to mark the site where Lopez turned onions into gold, referring to the tree under which he sought shade as the Oak of the Golden Dream. The area is now part of Placerita Canyon Park in Newhall.

MAKING WHOOPIE LEGAL
Rolling Hills

The city of Rolling Hills was only trying to rid its books of an arcane law when, instead, the exclusive community of fewer than 2,000 residents unwittingly garnered national headlines as the town that made adultery legal.

In the spring of 2003, city officials discovered a forty-six-year-old statute that made bedroom passions outside of marriage punishable by a $250 fine and three months in jail. The statute, the second one adopted by the city after it was incorporated in 1957, banned residents from "appealing to or gratifying the lust or passions or sexual desires of any person to whom he or she is not married." The law was also very specific about where such transgressions could not take place, outlawing sexual liaisons "in any bed, room, automobile, structure or public place."

Rolling Hills officials couldn't recall the statute ever being enforced and acknowledged that it was probably moot anyway, because the state took over jurisdiction in such personal matters following a court ruling in 1962. So it only made sense for the five happily married members of the Rolling Hills City Council to do away with the law, which they did. But the story of the vote, which was picked up by national media outlets, portrayed the city as voting to make adultery legal.

Of course, repeal of the law didn't mean that adulterers were going to get off free. It just meant that they would have to face a much sterner judgment from the authorities at home.

A VINTAGE VINE WITH A GREAT BOUQUET
Sierra Madre

In 1894 Alice Brugman needed a fast-growing plant for the front of her house and spent 75 cents on a Chinese lavender wisteria vine. Millions of blossoms, a world record, and more than one hundred years later, the plant is still growing.

Henry Fennel, an early owner of the house who inherited the quick-blooming plant, told neighbors that on hot summer nights he could actually *hear* the vine growing. By the 1930s Fennel saw that the vine had enveloped the residence and that he was headed for a showdown. "One of us is going to have to go," he declared. So he moved out and built another house 200 feet away and then watched as the unstoppable plant eventually collapsed the roof of the old house.

Maybe that's why some residents in this town refer to the giant wisteria as the Monster. Others are more gracious, labeling it the Lavender Lady or Queen of the San Gabriels. A lot of history has taken place under its spreading branches, which now measure more than 500 feet long in some spots. The incredible creeping plant has outlasted several owners. In 1990 it was recognized by the *Guinness Book of World Records* as the world's largest blossoming plant.

Sierra Madre has held a festival in its honor since 1918. Hundreds of visitors flock to the town each spring to check out booths with food and arts and crafts downtown and then trudge up the hill to see the famous giant vine. With so much invested in the plant, it's no wonder that the city spent up to $100,000 on "horticultural restoration" in the 1940s and 1960s to revive the plant, including injections of Vitamin B and hormones and the application of dry-ice packs.

A good vine improves with age.

The plant now produces more than 1.5 million blossoms each spring and weighs more than 250 tons. At each festival hundreds of locals outfit themselves head to toe in purple garb while visitors pose for pictures under the massive vine and wander among its fragrant blossoms.

For information about the Wisteria Festival, contact the Sierra Madre Chamber of Commerce at (626) 355–5111 or visit the Web site at www.sierramadrenews.net.

A LOT MORE THAN 99 BOTTLES OF BEER ON HER WALLS
Simi Valley

Tressa "Grandma" Prisbrey admitted that she couldn't draw a cow and make it look like a cow. She also knew that artistic vision could take many forms.

In 1956, when she was sixty years old and retired, she began building a structure to house her collection of 17,000 commemorative pencils, and she did it in a unique way. Her building materials were glass containers and mortar. So began Grandma's Prisbrey's bottle village, one of the country's most unusual examples of folk art.

Working through 1983, Prisbrey built more than two dozen structures in her own way, recycling more than one million bottles to create a quirky village of different-colored glass containers. She also built decorative pathways with embedded items such as license plates, tools, and assorted kitchen items. She even made a fence of television tubes and fashioned a tree out of pencils.

Prisbrey, who died in 1988 at age ninety-two, was fond of saying that anyone could make something with a million dollars, but that it takes more than money to make something out of nothing. Unfortunately, money is what's needed now to save her bottle village. Prisbrey received widespread recognition in the early 1980s as a visionary folk artist, and her village was listed on the National Register of Historic Places, only one of nine folk-art structures to receive this designation. All this recognition may do little to save her work, however. It was damaged in the 1994 Northridge earthquake and has languished ever since. A nonprofit committee hoping to save the structure has been trying to raise the necessary funds. You can contribute to the cause by visiting their Web site and adopting a square foot of the property. The Web site is echomatic.home .mindspring.com/bv/help.html.

A Blessing for the Buick and Other Vintage Cars
Sylmar

It has been well documented that the adoration of the automobile often reaches the level of religious fervor in Southern California. It's evident in the way some car owners spend hours polishing their vehicle's exterior to an exquisite finish, or how others pray to get just a few more miles out of a worn transmission.

It was truly fitting then for Stephanie and Gabriel Baltierra, who share a passion for vintage cars, to create an event that unites church ritual with vehicular ownership. The husband-and-wife team launched the Blessing of the Cars in 1993.

The event, held each summer in Sylmar's Hansen Dam Park, has become quite the thing for car lovers worldwide. It's open to pre-1968 cars and motorcycles, drawing thousands of hot rods, coupes, sedans, and other classic cars and their owners for a day of music and auto worship. The event officially begins with a mass blessing from a priest, who then goes car to car offering a more personalized prayer for each vehicle. Sometimes holy water is poured into radiators, if requested.

The event is also a car show and a chance for enthusiasts to show off their prized cars and earn awards, such as best custom car, best hot rod, best hard-luck story, and best of show.

For more information visit www.blessingofthecars.com or call (323) 663–1265.

A FLOWER MOST FOUL

*W*hile some botanists favor certain flowers for their beauty or pleasing aroma, the folks at the Huntington Botanical Gardens in San Marino cultivate one rare plant for its gross stench. Blooms from the Amorphophallus titanum, *the world's largest flower, are extremely rare in the United States. When they do occur, they create quite a sensation, and a tremendous stink as well, so much so that the plant's nickname is the corpse flower. Some people describe the bloom's scent as that of a dead horse; others compare the funky fragrance to rotting trash. One seven-year-old girl inhaled, then told a newspaper reporter, "It's like a bunch of gross stuff."*

But gross sells, or at least draws a crowd. When the Huntington's corpse flower bloomed in 1999, eager visitors couldn't wait to get a whiff of its horrible bouquet. The normally tranquil Huntington was suddenly reminiscent of Disneyland, with patrons snaking their way through a two-hour line to savor their moment of nightmarish smelling.

The same flower bloomed again in 2002, drawing thousands more grossed-out patrons and establishing Huntington's corpse flower as a rare plant indeed. Only twelve corpse flowers have bloomed in the United States in more than a century. Usually it takes each plant up to seven years before its trademark, and pungent, purple towering spear emerges.

In its native Sumatra, where the corpse flower is common, the reeking bloom is designed to attract pollinating dung beetles. Huntington officials caution that corpse plant's blooms are infrequent. But if you're in the neighborhood and smell something horrible, it might be worth stopping by at 1511 Oxford Road. Call ahead (626) 405–2100.

This flower by any other name would still stink.

Photo: The Huntington.

FRANK LEGAL COUNSEL
Van Nuys

There are plenty of places to get a hot dog in Southern California, but only one where along with your wiener you can also get some wise legal advice on the side. Law Dogs has been a Valley tradition since attorney Kim Pearman opened it in 1981. Like other hot-dog stands, you can get a variety of links here, along with onions, chili, and other toppings. The bonus is that each Wednesday starting at 7:00 P.M., patrons at the stand can munch on their dogs and line up for a free legal consultation with Pearman or one of several participating attorneys.

Pearman tells folks that he isn't in for the money—in his private practice he can earn $250 an hour. He thinks of Law Dogs as a valuable service for those who need free legal help, as well as providing a nice diversion from his regular work. With the aroma of well-seasoned links wafting about, Pearman holds court in the back of the stand and fields a variety of legal queries, ranging from the mundane to more thorny issues of child-visitation rights and sticky divorce proceedings.

Pearman's five other Law Dogs around the Valley closed when business tailed off. He blames it more on changing dietary habits, with people eating fewer hot dogs, rather than a failed concept of trying to run a legal-aid service in the back of a food stand.

Now only the original stand remains, a unique service truly relished by persons hungry for a good dog and good advice.

Law Dogs is located at 14114 Sherman Way and can be reached by phone at (818) 908–3234.

HOG HEAVEN
Vernon

If pigs had a paradise, it would look much like what's depicted on the walls of an industrial plant in Vernon: hogs frolicking by a stream while a boy fishes nearby, smiling hogs playfully upending a farmer, or hogs romping in mud or galloping through tall grass.

Don't judge a meatpacking plant by its walls.

The irony here is that this 30,000-square-foot mural of pleasurable pigs covers the Farmer John meatpacking plant. Inside, of course, it's a different story. The plant slaughters hundreds of pigs daily and turns them into a variety of pork products, most famously, Dodger Dogs.

When the Farmer John plant was opened in 1931 by the Clougherty brothers, this area was crammed with slaughterhouses and packing plants. In 1957 the brothers commissioned Hollywood scenic painter Leslie Grimes to cover a wall with a mural, and Grant had the idea to make a series of whimsical farm scenes featuring blissful hogs. The brothers liked it and asked him to cover the exterior of the entire plant, and for the next eleven years Grimes worked on the murals until he died from a scaffolding fall. Artist Arno Jordan picked up where Grimes left off, and by the 1980s virtually every building in the eleven-acre facility was covered. The murals were given a major restoration in 2000 by artist Philip Slagter, and they remain a popular tourist destination. A hint: Visit on the weekends. Vernon is an industrial town that draws thousands of people during the week but fewer than 200 families live there on the weekends, when you can easily get a close-up look at this unique conception of a rural fantasy.

The plant is located at 3049 East Vernon Avenue. For more information you can visit the company's Web site at www.farmerjohn.com.

CEMENTING HIS VISION OF PIONEER LIFE
Woodland Hills

Boot Hill exists only in the imagination of self-taught artist John Ehn. As he conjured it up in his outsized, colorful cement sculptures and backdrops, it looks like a wild and whimsical Old West town. There's the cemetery with funny gravestone epitaphs such as that belonging to Red Finn, who suffocated on a gin cork but "died in good spirits." There's the grave of Big Foot Brown, a six-toed giant who's not even below ground yet and who wears an invitation on his sleeve that reads: SHAKE MY HAND, GIRLS, I AIN'T BEEN DEAD LONG.

Ehn was a former government trapper who came to California in the early 1940s and eventually opened a lodge near the Burbank Airport. From 1951 until his death in 1981, he made his Old West sculptures, modeling them after family members and friends, and then displaying them at his hotel, which he called The Old Trapper's Lodge. Most of the sculptures reflect Ehn's pioneer spirit and frontier sense of humor, whereas some have a more gruesome tone, such as the battle between Pegleg Smith and Big Bear, in which the pair is depicted in a bloody confrontation, apparently over a cow they both think they own. Family members have said that this work is meant as a fable extolling the values of sharing.

The state declared Ehn's sculptures a historical landmark, but after his death it was hard to find a place willing to display them. Finally, Pierce College gave them a home, setting them up in a park near a campus building. Surviving family and friends, however, perform the required maintenance to make sure the works remain in good shape.

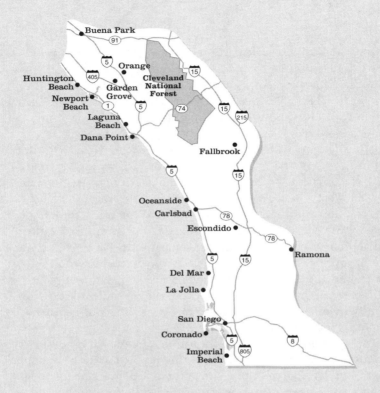

ORANGE COAST AND SAN DIEGO REGION

Orange Coast and San Diego Region

A CELEBRITY CAST OF WAX
Buena Park

The figures at the Movieland Wax Museum sure look like Hollywood stars. They just can't act. Or move at all, for that matter.

Allen Parkinson got the urge to create a waxy Hollywood tribute after a 1958 visit to Madame Tussaud's wax palace in London. He launched Movieland in 1962 with a premiere that had all the glitz of a Hollywood movie opening. Screen-legend Mary Pickford cut the ceremonial ribbon.

A most excellent adventure in wax. Photo: Movieland Wax Museum.

Though Parkinson died in 2002, his museum continues to add new stars to its cast. Lifelike figures of Bruce Willis, Julia Roberts, Arnold Schwarzenegger, Madonna, Jim Carrey, and others make up the 300 famous people displayed here. Not surprisingly, the stars closely monitor the creation of their wax persona, ensuring that it meets their standard. They even submit to detailed measurements and donate wardrobe items for a more authentic look.

If you want a chance to hang out with more stars than show up at an Oscar party, head to the Movieland Wax Museum at 7711 Beach Boulevard, a block north of Knott's Berry Farm. The phone number is (714) 522–1155. You can also check out www.movielandwaxmuseum.com.

IT'S A SMALL PLASTIC WORLD AFTER ALL
Carlsbad

In the 1967 film *The Graduate,* scrub-faced college-grad Benjamin Braddock, played by Dustin Hoffman, is told that his future can be summed up in one word: plastics. The advice is offered with comic irony in the film, but it begs the question: What would the world look like if it were all plastic? The answer is LEGOLAND.

California's LEGOLAND, which opened in 1999, consists of 128 acres built up with 30 million Lego pieces, a shrine to the construction possibilities of the brightly colored interlocking plastic blocks known as Legos. California's LEGOLAND is the only one of its kind in America, although there are three other LEGOLANDs in Europe.

The park offers rides and other fun stuff for kids, but the most fascinating section is Miniland. This area features plastic-

A government for the peewee and by the peewee.
Photo: LEGOLAND.

constructed miniature versions of American landmarks and
cities such as the Golden Gate Bridge, New Orleans, Washington, D.C., Manhattan, and a New England harbor. These models
sport sophisticated animations that include lights at the Hollywood Bowl that change to the music, a whirring presidential
helicopter on the White House lawn, break-dancers on the
streets of Manhattan, and a cops-and-robber chase on a Los
Angeles rooftop.

The model of the U.S. Capitol consists of 1.6 million bricks
and weighs 717 pounds, which makes you wonder whether the
future-as-plastic prophecy in *The Graduate* was as hollow as
you would first think.

For more information visit the company Web site at
www.lego.com and follow the links to LEGOLAND in California
or just drive over to One Legoland Drive in Carlsbad.

SEEING THE WORLD THROUGH
RANUNCULUS-COLORED GLASSES
Carlsbad

Most Americans grew up hearing about the agricultural
exploits of Johnny Appleseed, who roamed the America
wilderness planting apple seeds. A lesser-known horticulture
revolutionary was Luther Gage, whose planting passion wasn't
apples but a colorful flower native to Asia Minor known as the
'Tecolote' ranunculus, or the Persian buttercup.

Gage introduced ranunculus flower seeds to North American
in the 1930s, and that first planting would eventually lead to the
creation of one of the most stunning flower fields in America.

The ranunculus thrived in the temperate Southern California
climate, a fact noticed by a worker hired by Gage, Frank
Frazee. Soon Frazee and his family started the first commercial
ranunculus farm in America. The many colorful varieties of
the flower created a dazzling roadside view as the flower farm
was visible from the nearby highway. Motorists taken by the
spectacle would literally stop to smell the flowers.

That blooming hillside of radiant pink, purple, yellow, and
other glowing tones is now officially known as the Flower
Fields. Each spring almost a quarter million visitors show up
just for the thrill of walking among the flowers. More than six
million tubers are harvested here annually and are available for
sale, along with fresh cut flowers and potted plants.

Though the flowers are enough of an artwork by themselves, the owners of the fields began a program in 2000 to

commission artists to create works using the flowers as their medium.

Flower viewing is usually from early March through early May. The entrance is at 5704 Paseo Del Norte. Admission is charged. For more information call (760) 431–0352 or visit them on the Web at www.theflowerfields.com.

Not Afraid of a Little Ghostly Publicity
Coronado

If there were rumors of a ghost rattling around a swanky hotel, especially one where rooms come at a premium and guests are there to relax in Victorian comfort, you'd expect management to do its best to sweep those spirited tales under the fancy carpeting. That's why it's hard to figure the folks at Hotel Del Coronado, who have gone out of their way to publicize an eerie tale of a haunting that has spooked guests at the landmark seaside hotel for decades and continues to jangle nerves.

In 2002 the hotel published *Beautiful Stranger: The Ghost of Kate Morgan and the Hotel del Coronado,* an account of the mysterious and attractive spirit who has haunted the fancy hotel for more than a century. The book was written by hotel-historian Christine Donovan and is available in the hotel's gift shop.

The historical account recalls Morgan's ill-fated stay at the hotel in 1898. She arrived without luggage, registered under a false name, and was found shot to death a few days later. Her dramatic demise generated a swirl of media attention and was ultimately ruled a suicide. Stories circulated that she was pregnant and abandoned by her husband, and some witnesses

Ghostly, but fashionable. Photo: Hotel del Coronado.

reported that she had had a lover's spat with her spouse on the train ride to the hotel. He never checked in with his wife.

Ever since Morgan's death, the room she stayed in, now number 3327, has been the scene of the usual ghostly shenanigans, including flickering lights, rattling doorknobs, and bedcovers snatched off in the middle of the night. Morgan's ghost appears to be more prankster than evil spirit, according to Donovan's book, which also includes the transcript of the coroner's inquest, a copy of Morgan's 1892 death certificate, and a page from the hotel registry the day she signed in. Morgan also appears to be a restless spirit, as paranormal activity has been witnessed in other rooms, as well as in hallways and along the beach. Enjoy your stay!

The hotel is located on the water at 1500 Orange Avenue, or you can visit the hotel's Web site at www.hoteldel.com or phone (888) 236–1357.

T O E S   O N   T H E   N O S E
D a n a   P o i n t

For Bob Howard, "hang ten" is more that just a surfing expression; it's a romantic mission. He has devoted years and thousands of dollars in his quest to develop a revolutionary surfboard that would allow surfers precious more seconds on the tip of their boards, their ten toes hanging over the edge in a position surfers say is the most exhilarating way to ride.

"Riding the nose is just pure ecstasy. And if you can add a couple of seconds of that ecstasy, well, you never want to stop ecstasy," he explains.

In trying to create a new surfboard, Howard is definitely going against the current. First there were long boards, and then there were short boards, and very little innovation in

Bob Howard is making waves with a new board design.
Photo: Louise Howard.

board design in between. But Howard is convinced he can create a board that would reward serious noseriders with the rides of their lives.

He remembers, as a kid, surfing in Huntington Beach one day when he spotted surfer Tom Morey with a board he had designed for noseriding. It was unusually wide and thick, different from any other board Howard had seen. "It was like a UFO had landed. It was very exciting to me. I have never forgotten that," he says.

Howard's first noseriding board of his own design was made in 1994. He called it the Koanda because he based its design on physics principles developed by a Romanian scientist with that name. Howard crafted a domed attachment that would theoretically create more suction on the board's tail and make it behave, he says, so that noseriders would have a more stable platform on which to operate. Howard says the board was proven successful when professional surfer Israel Paskowitz rode it to get 16.5 seconds of noseriding at a contest in Ventura.

Howard's latest board is called the Flat Fish Noserider, which observers say looks like a bowling pin sliced in half. Despite its appearance surfers who have used it say it rides the nose like crazy.

Howard's boards, and an ocean of information on noseriding, are available at his Web site, www.noseriding.com.

Minding Their Own Beeswax
Del Mar

A factory fire in 1983 almost caused the longtime Knorr family candle business to go up in smoke. After the fire family members talked about closing down the candle shop, which had opened in 1928. But Steve Knorr, grandson of the founder, decided to assume ownership, and he has kept the family flame alive. Since taking over, Steve has made the shop the country's largest producer of 100-percent beeswax candles. In all, the chandlery transforms more than a million pounds of beeswax into candles each year.

Some of the candles have made it to the big screen, featured in films such as *Interview with a Vampire* and *Practical Magic*. Others have decorated tables at the White House.

That's quite a feat for a company that traces its roots to a sideline by founder Ferdinand Knorr, who ran a tool-and-die shop and cultivated bees as a hobby. He sold some of his first candles to the Rancho Sante Fe Inn, and guests there liked them so much they stopped by to buy their own. Now the store sells worldwide through catalogs and the Internet and even features one candle that burns at both ends. For more information call (858) 755–2051 or visit the shop's Web site at www.knorrcandleshop.com or the shop itself, which is at 14906 Via De La Valle, off I–5.

A TRULY WUNNERFUL PLACE
Escondido

Though Disneyland may lay claim to being the happiest place on earth, visitors who venture to this paradise of polka music and golf might differ. The sprawling Welk Resort draws vacationing families and busloads of true believers who come to pay tribute to Lawrence Welk, the accordion player and band leader whose long-running television show beamed images of a happy and squeaky-clean America. His music and onstage demeanor were so light and frothy that Welk became known as the King of Champagne Music.

A LITTLE HELP FROM ABOVE

*T*he world is not a perfect place, of course, and loads of people have ideas about fixing things. A group of UFO believers in El Cajon, a few miles east of San Diego, are counting on some outside help to solve problems such as pollution, dwindling energy supplies, and other global concerns. That's really *outside* help, as in from another planet.

The folks at the Unarius Academy of Science believe that really smart aliens from a planet called Myton are gearing up for an Earth landing, and the academy can't wait until they get here. That's because Unarius followers believe that Myton inhabitants, called Muons, will graciously become role models for Earthlings and help us create a better world. Not only that, they'll be consultants for past-life therapy.

The academy was founded in 1954 by Ernest and Ruth Norman, who have since gone on to their higher beings. Unarius, by the way, is an acronym for Universal Articulate Interdimensional Understanding of Science. Originally the projected arrival of the Muons was 2001, but the date passed without a revolutionary encounter from outer space. That hasn't dampened spirits at the academy, however, where officials report that contact has been made with the Muons and they're close by, just waiting for the right moment to land. The group suggests that the power of positive thinking might encourage them to make their friendly invasion.

In the meantime the group holds regular cosmically themed lectures and events. You can stop by for a visit, at 145 South Magnolia Avenue, or contact them at (800) 475–7062. Or you can have a close encounter with the group in cyberspace by visiting www.unarius.org.

The resort that bears his name is, as he might say, "wunner-ful." It has a spa, an 18-hole golf course, and a theater that specializes in productions where no one utters curses. The real treat for Welk fans is the museum, which holds the world's largest champagne glass, measured at 6 feet high and 5 feet across, which was given to Welk on the anniversary of his twenty-fifth year in television. Other exhibits include Welk's personalized golf cart and a life-size replica of his bandstand set. Visitors can also view memorabilia from his life and scenes of his North Dakota childhood. Outside the museum is a life-size bronze statue of Welk with his arms raised, baton in hand. You can almost hear his trademark countdown: "Uh-one and uh-two . . . "

The museum is located in the lobby of the resort theater at 8860 Lawrence Welk Drive. The theater box office can be reached by calling (888) 802–7469.

A FESTIVAL THAT DRAWS LOTS OF DIPS
Fallbrook

It's no secret what keeps the town of Fallbrook humming along: It's the avocados. Avocado trees were first planted here in 1912, and now the town's hundreds of small avocado groves generate more than $70 million in annual revenue. Fallbrook's designation as the Avocado Capital of the World is hard earned, an honor celebrated since the mid-1980s with an avocado festival.

There's plenty of guacamole dip at the fair for sure, with pros and amateurs alike competing for best-recipe awards. Other contests are more intriguing, such as the Avo Olympics, which features intense competition in avocado-pit spitting and avocado croquet. Then there's the Avocado 500, where contestants outfit avocados with wheels to see which fruit is the fastest. Car crashes here are no problem—they're just scooped up with tortilla chips. Most peculiar of all, perhaps, is the contest to determine the best-dressed and best-decorated avocados.

It's no surprise that the avocado-themed town has a number of Mexican restaurants. One, La Caseta, decided in 1992 to make one heck of a superburrito. It weighed 2,237 pounds and measured 3 feet wide and 36 feet long, establishing a world record that it held for a few years. Fortunately, the town had enough guacamole around to complement the supersize entree.

For more information about the avocado festival, visit the town's Web site at www.fallbrookca.org or call (760) 728–5845.

Gourdeous Art
Fallbrook

Doug Welburn grows a vegetable nobody eats, yet he's a successful farmer. That's because he harvests gourds, hard-shelled vegetables that usually end up in art galleries, not on dinner plates.

"Very few people have attempted to eat them," Welburn says of his gourd crop. Although they belong to the same family as more edible varieties such as pumpkins and squash, gourds are unique. After harvest their shells become hard, like wood, instead of rotting. "No other vegetable does that," Welburn says.

The hard surface becomes a canvas for legions of vegetable artists who turn the gourds into something worthy of display, not digestion. Welburn says that one decorative gourd sold for $21,000, but most are priced between $30 and $50.

Hard-shell gourds have been around for centuries throughout the world, Welburn points out. "Some have been found in the pyramids in Egypt," he says. He plants several different

THE SEXIEST FISH ALIVE

*T*he strangest mating ritual displayed in Southern
California doesn't occur in the region's many
trendy bars but rather on sandy beaches at night,
mostly in spring and summer. The romantics in question are tiny silvery fish known as grunion.

On certain nights, shortly after high tide, grunion
suddenly in the mood are compelled to embark on a
massive spawning that can be described only as a
fishy love-in. Females lead the charge onto the beach
and drill themselves into the sand with their heads
up, releasing eggs a few inches below the surface.
Males show up a few seconds later to fertilize the
eggs, and then they're gone, quickly followed by the
females.

If conditions are right, beaches are sometimes lit-
tered with thousands of the frisky grunion, which
measure about 5 inches in length. Grunion are the
only known fish who lay their eggs on land.

But that's not the most unusual sight on these
nights. Rather, it's the people who show up to hunt the
grunion. Armed with sacks and flashlights, they dart
around the beach looking for the stranded ones,
snatching up as many as they can before the fish are
washed back into the sea by the next wave. It's legal to
catch grunion while they are on the beach, but you
can only use your bare hands. It's a ritual all its own,
and many people use the annual grunion run as an
excuse to have a beach party. Some of the best spots
for grunion hunting are along beaches in Orange and
San Diego Counties, including Huntington Beach,
Newport Beach, Corona del Mar, Del Mar, La Jolla,
and Mission Beach.

Doug Welburn and his horde of gourds.
Photo: Courtesy Welburn Gourd Farm.

types of seeds that produce gourds as puny as a peanut and as substantial as 3 feet across. They grow to maturity in six months and then take another six months to "cure out," or dry.

Welburn claims that his gourd farm is the world's largest producer of this unique vegetable, distributing more than 300,000 each year. To celebrate this distinction, the farm hosts an annual gourd festival where visitors can marvel at hundreds of examples of gourd art and can even attend classes that show novice vegetable artists how to get started. There are plenty of vegetables you can eat there as well, and music and fun stuff for kids. For more information call (760) 728–4271 or visit the farm's Web site at www.welburngourdfarm.com.

S E R M O N   O N   T H E   M O U N T E D   J U M B O T R O N
Garden Grove

The Reverend Dr. Robert Schuller always had a flair for the dramatic. He arrived in Garden Grove in 1955 and began preaching from atop a snack bar in the local drive-in theater, which is believed to be California's first drive-in church. But the Reverend Schuller had a dream to build a great church, and what he created here is nothing short of a grand fusion of religion and theater.

Members of the Crystal Cathedral Congregation don't have to wait until services start to be awed; they merely look around. The cathedral, dedicated in 1980, is said to be the largest glass building in the world, a star-shaped edifice that contains more than 10,000 windows of tempered silver-colored glass. The massive 90-foot doors behind the marble altar open automatically, as if on orders from above, to let in light and outdoor breezes. A massive bell tower has a fifty-two-bell carillon. The pipe organ, which has 16,000 pipes, is one of the five largest in the world.

The main church holds close to 3,000 worshipers in comfortable theater-style seating. A Sony Jumbotron screen broadcasts the entire service for persons seated too far back. People can also follow the service in an outdoor viewing area while remaining comfortably in their car.

Services are broadcast worldwide as the *Hour of Power* show, which has attracted such celebrities as Charlton Heston and Arnold Schwarzenegger.

The church's Easter passion play and its *Splendor of Christmas* are elaborately staged affairs that would make any theater producer proud. The Christmas show features the pageantry of live animals, including camels, parading through the aisles, and the spectacle of flying angels soaring overhead. It's enough to keep even less enthusiastic congregational members on the edge of their seats.

The Crystal Cathedral, located at 12141 Lewis Street, offers tours. For more information call (714) 971–4013 or visit the church's Web site at www.crystalcathedral.org.

A DARK BRANCH OF HISTORY

With a magnificent dense grove of oak trees and numerous recreational opportunities such as nature trails, ball fields, and picnic tables, Felicita Park in Escondido certainly lives up to its name as a joyous place. Yet a horrific legend haunts the spot.

Now kids frolic in the massive and magnificently shaped branches of the park's oak trees, but local lore has it that shrieks of agony once rang out from this very orchard of natural beauty. Native Poway Indians referred to this area as the Judgment Grove, as they handed out truly harsh penalties to tribal members found guilty of certain crimes, including cowardice. The tale goes that victims were bound to and suspended from the trees for years in a hellish tree prison. The oaks thus earned the name of the "torture trees."

Though some historians have cast doubt on the story, the city presents the account on its Web site as the truth. Meanwhile the trees, some of which are hundreds of years old, aren't talking.

A L L   T H E S E   D U C K S   A R E N ' T   I N   A   R O W
Huntington Beach

Every year thousands of spectators gather on the sands of this beach town to watch an ocean race involving hundreds of swimmers making a made dash to the finish line. That's the idea, anyway, of the annual Duck-a-thon charity event, where hundreds of rubber ducks are dumped into the ocean from the Huntington Beach Pier to see which one makes it to shore first. Each ducky has a paid sponsor, but it's hard to root for your favorite, because they all look alike, aside from an identification number.

The annual race debuted in 1992 and now raises more than $100,000 for the Huntington Beach Community Clinic. Participants purchase a standard yellow rubber ducky for a small fee and receive a certificate as an entrant. It takes the ducks about thirty minutes to reach shore. They're scooped up and their order of finish duly recorded, with top duck owners getting donated prizes, including travel vouchers, free meals, and entertainment tickets.

"It's sort of a family affair. People come out and picnic and watch their ducks come in," says Pat Davis, who clearly enjoys her role as organizer of the event. For a bit more money, you can enter a special duck that rides a tiny surfboard. But the secret's out: The surfing ducks don't travel any faster than their swimming counterparts.

The Duck-a-thon is held over a weekend in the middle of May and features vendor booths and food in addition to the race. The regular race is held on Saturday; corporate-sponsored ducks race Sunday to win the coveted Golden Duck Award. For more information call (714) 374–1951, or visit the Duck-a-thon's, er, Web site: www.duck-a-thon.org.

Rubber ducks take the plunge. Photo: Courtesy of the Duck-a-thon.

BONE APPETIT
Huntington Beach

Michael Bartusick's restaurant is going to the dogs. Literally. But he wouldn't have it any other way.

The Park Bench Cafe, the restaurant he has owned since 1988 with his wife, Christie, offers tasty standard breakfast and lunch fare. But turn the menu over and you notice a sec-

Hot Diggity Dog anyone?

tion called Canine Cuisine, which is where this restaurant radically diverges from traditional eateries. Here are entrees to whet the appetites of pooches, not people, including the popular Hot Diggity Dog, an all-beef hot dog without the bun cut into doggie-bite pieces, and Chilly Paws, a single scoop of vanilla ice cream for that pampered pet. Eight different choices are served in disposable bowls so as not to run afoul of local health ordinances.

The doggie menu, Bartusick says, "kind of created itself." At first, because of the restaurant's location in a park, many customers were people who stopped with their pets for refreshment after recreational romps. Some customers would sneak their tired pooches some water or table scraps, and restaurant help were willing accomplices. The first thing Bartusick did was set up a water tank with bowls to offer pets a drink. The menu just made everything official. He tries to keep it simple, offering basic meat dishes and biscuit treats. "We're not going to go crazy and start making omelets for dogs," he claims.

Dogs are clearly welcome here, but there's little tolerance for bad doggie behavior, like jumping on tables or chairs. Dogs who act out can be banished to the doghouse and deprived of dining privileges.

The Park Bench Cafe, located at 17732 Golden West Street, can be reached by calling (714) 842-0775.

IT'S CULTURE, DUDE!
Huntington Beach

As a beach city with a longstanding reputation as a world surfing capital, Huntington Beach certainly takes great pride in its designation as Surf City U.S.A. Hawaiian Duke Kahanamoku, revered as the father of the sport, surfed the waves around the city's pier in the 1920s, and U.S. surfing championships have been held here for decades.

Two nonsurfers, however, led the drive to help create and maintain the city's most visible tribute to the sport, the Huntington Beach International Surfing Museum, which opened in 1987. Natalie Kotsch, a local real-estate broker, helped found the museum, and Ann Beasley, a native of West Virginia, is its head docent.

Though the museum has an international label, it has a quaint interior, but plans are taking shape to move the museum into a bigger space and to expand its scope. Now housed in an Art Deco building a short walk from the city's pier, the museum features exhibits that detail legends of the sport and its associ-

Which way to the water?

ated culture. All board sports are displayed here, including skateboarding, represented by a wall of boards that traces the evolution of the skateboard through past decades.

A bust of Duke Kahanamoku dominates the museum's opening section, and another exhibit documents the successful drive to have a U.S. postage stamp issued in 2002 in his honor. In a back section clips from popular surfing movies are played and available for viewing. There are dozens of photographs featuring legends of the sport, including many local surfing kings, and a wall dedicated to women surfers.

One section documents the birth of surf music, which the museum traces to a Huntington Beach ballroom, since burned down, and the music of Dick Dale and the Del-Tones back in 1961.

Other unusual items relate to skin diving and spear fishing, with a set of bamboo goggles and a spear gun from the 1930s, and a timeline and artifacts tracing the history of spear fishing in America.

All of which should make any surfer shout: "Cowabunga!"

The International Surfing Museum is located at 411 Olive Avenue and can be reached by calling (714) 960–3483. Surf over to the museum's Web site at www.surfingmuseum.org.

QUICKLY FADING BEAUTY
Imperial Beach

Anyone who has ever made a crude castle in the sand using a plastic bucket knows the main drawback to toiling at this creative effort: It only lasts until the tide rolls in. What may be considered a museum piece one moment is rudely reduced to muddy rubble in what has to be the most temporary of art forms.

The fleeting beauty of sand sculpture unfolds on a grand scale at this border beach city, which hosts the annual U.S. Open Sandcastle Competition every July. The event attracts more than a quarter million spectators and dozens of artists who envision sand works that go well beyond the mere pail-and-shovel creations of most amateurs. These are soaring, detailed projects that dazzle the crowd—that is, until the tide does its dirty work and all the magnificent art recedes back to measly wet sand.

But for those few moments, the spectacle of this competition, considered the biggest and best of those held around the country, is truly great. Past creations include replicas of San Francisco's Transamerica Building, a giant sand maze negotiated by a live mouse, and a larger-than-life depiction of the god Neptune frolicking in a hot tub with two mermaids.

Participants say that what makes this contest special is the unique quality of the sand on the beach, which is very conducive to sculpting. It holds its shape well, allowing sand artists to realize their most vivid designs.

The event is noteworthy enough that city officials have fashioned a full weekend of festivities around it, including the Sandcastle Ball on Friday, a Saturday parade, and a kids' competition followed by evening fireworks, all culminating on Sunday morning with the Sandcastle Open. Look quickly. As the sun begins to fade that weekend, even the most glorious creations will be nothing more than a memory.

For dates of the annual event, call (619) 424–3151 or visit the Imperial Beach Chamber of Commerce Web site at www.ib-chamber.org.

IT'S BOTTOMS UP AT THIS ANNUAL EVENT

*A*mtrak travelers along the coastal route in California have loads of interesting scenery to contemplate as they make their journey. Once a year, though, passengers are treated to an especially breathtaking sight as the train zooms through Laguna Niguel: a massive mooning by pants-dropping celebrants at a local tavern.

The town's annual Moon-Fest is out of character for this normally buttoned-down community. But even conservatives need to let off some steam sometimes or, at least, air out their backsides. The unusual tradition began in the late 1970s. Legend has it that a patron at the Mugs Away tavern was celebrating his birthday and offered free drinks to anyone who would expose his or her caboose to trains that pass within a few yards of the bar. Dignity lost out to the prospect of free refreshments as a few friends took him up on the offer. Next year, the tradition continued, and it has grown ever since, drawing a few thousand flashers in recent years in what has to be a world's record for mooning a train, if such things are indeed noted.

Participants arrive at sunrise to gear up, or down, as the case may be. A train schedule is posted outside the bar so that mooning opportunities are duly observed throughout the day. There are plenty of chances. Two trains pass by each hour, beginning at 7:30 in the morning until close to midnight. Vendors sell T-shirts to commemorate the event, and a handy Web site (www.moonamtrak.org) offers tips, a train schedule, and a little background to guide would-be train flashers, who include some local politicians.

For the record Amtrak officials have tried to distance themselves from the event, preferring to turn the other cheek.

LIFE IMITATING ART
Laguna Beach

Some artists work to make their creations resemble real life. Creative types in this artist colony strive for the exact opposite: to transform real life into a flattened canvas. The annual Pageant of the Masters, held during this city's summer-arts festival, turns three-dimensional actors into two-dimensional works of classical and contemporary art.

More than just a gag, this full-time operation requires months of planning, rehearsal, stage building, and costume designing. Hundreds of people turn out to audition each winter as festival planners take their measurements and pictures and select those most likely to portray figures in a particular painting. Actors are costumed and painted to look as flat as possible and then posed against giant backdrops.

Each year about three dozen paintings and sculptures are re-created this way and are presented to gasping audiences in the popular production. Orchestral accompaniment adds to the drama. The artworks re-created each year are tied to a theme, with the only recurring work being *The Last Supper.*

To complete the illusion, actors must remain frozen for the few minutes they're posed as a painting, holding off itching or any other indication that they're actually real.

For information visit the festival's Web site at www.foapom .com or call (800) 487–3378.

SURFING DUDETTES
La Jolla

As the sport of surfing grew in America, there was always a place for the girls: on the beach, looking good, watching the guys ride the waves. Eventually girls discovered that it was more fun to be in the water hanging ten than lounging around on the sandy sideline.

Isabelle "Izzy" Tihanyi and her twin sister, Caroline "Coco," were taught how to surf by their father when they were eight years old. They've both turned the sport into a lifelong passion.

"I've surfed pretty much every day of my life," says Izzy. "When I'm out in the water, it doesn't matter what's in my bank account. I'm not thinking of the millions of things I have to do. Surfing allows me the freedom to relax and focus on just having fun."

The sisters figured that other girls would be equally thrilled, so they opened the world's first surfing school for girls and women, Surf Diva. Now they introduce hundreds of women to the formerly male-dominated sport on the same beach where their father once paddled out with them for the first time.

"The perception that surfing is a guy's sport bothered me. I think it turns some women and girls off from even trying it out. Women are led to believe that they aren't strong, brave, or skilled enough to surf, and that they are lacking some key ingredient," says Izzy.

The school turns that all around with a support staff of talented women surfers and a line of Surf Diva clothing and accessories designed to make women feel proud of their surfing status. The school's motto is: "The best surfer in the water is the one having the most fun."

Izzy makes it look easy. Photo: Todd Peterson.

Boys aren't completely left out. Men are offered lessons in special classes called Boys on the Side. And when instruction is offered about surfing etiquette, divas are told not to snag a wave if another surfer has already taken it—unless, of course "he's really cute."

Surf Diva can be reached by calling (858) 454–8273. Information about classes can be found on its Web site at www.surfdiva.com.

MAKING IRRELEVANCE NOTEWORTHY
Newport Beach

It's perhaps fitting that when Paul Salata first launched Irrelevant Week back in 1976, no one much noticed. As events go, it was, well, pretty irrelevant. Salata's vision was a week of activities honoring the last player chosen in the National Football League college draft, a player with little chance of actually making it in professional sports.

That bothered Salata, who played football at the University of Southern California and as a pro for the 49ers and Colts. "Football is a team sport. Everyone talks about how you're only as good as the last man on the roster. Well, we decided to do something about it," Salata says.

With all the media and fan attention focused on the marquee players selected in the earlier rounds, Salata vowed to do something nice for the guy no one much noticed—the last of the last, an athlete chosen mostly as an afterthought because teams had to select someone. His plan was to show Mr. Irrelevant a good time. "We think laughing is a lot better than crying," Salata says.

Somehow, though, Irrelevant Week has blossomed into a tradition that's worth noting. Mr. Irrelevant has become relevant.

Oops! The Lowsman trophy is awarded to the football fumbler.
Photo: Courtesy of Irrelevant Week.

The annual event is now attended by many sports notables and is well covered by the media.

Each April, as the NFL draft concludes, much fanfare is generated when the final player is selected and designated Mr. Irrelevant. The NFL has gotten into the spirit of the celebration and invited Salata to announce the final pick each year.

The player is invited to Newport Beach in June to be honored for a week of activities in his honor. Mr. Irrelevant XXVI, tight end Tevita Ofahengaue, a Tongan raised in Hawaii who played college ball at Brigham Young University, was feted with an opening luau, followed by a week of special events, many which raised money for local charities.

Each year Irrelevant Week culminates in a banquet at which Mr. Irrelevant is presented with the Lowsman Trophy. The special award is Irrelevant Week's answer to the Heisman Trophy and features a player frozen in game action who is fumbling away the football, representing the nonachievement of the league's final draft pick.

For more information call (949) 263–0727.

HISTORY WITH A SIDE OF FRIES
Oceanside

Patrons dropping by the 101 Cafe certainly warm to the comfort food on the menu, including the variety of burgers and the chicken-fried steak or meatloaf dinner. But many drop by for a taste of something else: a rich slice of California coastal history.

The 101 Cafe is more than just a roadside diner; it's a living museum of what life was like a few decades ago along California's famed coastal route.

History 101: a cafe that looks back in time. Photo: Charlie Newman.

The cafe opened in 1928 as a twenty-seat diner serving hungry motorists along Highway 101, the former mother road of California that handled all coastal traffic. Although the cafe went through some remodeling and a couple of name changes through the years, it has been restored with its original name and look by current owner John Daley, who bought it in the late 1980s with a partner. There are original touches such as counter dining and comfy booths. "We even have the same style of waitressing—one waitress working her butt off and serving the whole restaurant and making sure everyone's happy," Daley says.

Daley, who grew up in Oceanside and has a strong interest in local history, has decorated the cafe's walls with historic photographs of Highway 101. Daley wants people to remember the rich history of the famed roadway, even though it's often bypassed now since the completion of Interstate 5 in the mid-1960s.

Some diners have been stopping by for decades. "They come here for the history," Daley says. And some pie, too.

The 101 Cafe is located at 631 South Coast Highway, and the phone number is (760) 722-5220. The restaurant's Web site, www.101cafe.net, includes many links to more information about Highway 101 history.

HERE COMES THE BRIDAL COLLECTION
Orange

The way Eve Faulkner sees it, modern women can learn a lot from the way courtship was conducted more than a century ago. "We've gone from formal dating and chaperones to heavy petting in the backseat of your boyfriend's car," she says. "It's crazy."

What happened to romance, sentimentality, and tradition? Faulkner's quest is to open up the eyes of women to the lost traditions of Victorian-era courtship and nuptials.

A few years back Faulkner began collecting antique wedding gowns and accessories and also researching wedding traditions. She now has fifty wedding gowns, dating from 1835 to 1925, that tell the story of a simpler, more refined era of getting hitched. Her collection, formerly housed in a Victorian-era home in Orange, is now a "museum on wheels," she says. Parts of the collection will be exhibited periodically at other museums. Meanwhile she takes some of her antique gowns with her as props when she lectures women on the value of a Victorian sentimentality when it comes to dating and picking a mate.

"Everything that the bride wore, from the top of her head to her undergarments, had a tradition and meaning behind it.

When I teach that to women today, their mouths just hang open. They love it," Faulkner says.

Faulkner illuminates a corseted world of silk and lace, wedding trousseaus, formal courting, and high teas, all done up in white-on-white splendor. She traces the tradition of a white wedding dress to Queen Victoria, who donned one made of white satin and Honiton lace. Though most of her antique bridal outfits here suggest memorable times long ago, the exhibit of the "gown that was never worn" tells the less-joyous story of a woman who bought a wedding dress but lost her groom before she could wear it.

Faulkner says she has seen the value of having traditions to count on in her own life. She was in Juvenile Hall when she was seventeen, the victim of a broken home. Later she and her husband ran a foster home for teenage girls. "All we had to offer them was a house filled with love and a strong foundation. Now many have gone on to successful careers and lives," Faulkner says.

For more information about Faulkner's collection and lecture schedule, call (714) 997–1893 or visit victorianbridalmuseum.com.

How Do You Milk a Camel? Very Carefully
Ramona

Camels have a nasty reputation as unruly beasts prone to spitting, so Gil Riegler would like to set the dromedary record straight.

"Camels are so intelligent and sensitive," he says. The first camel he encountered was part of a program that pairs animals with disabled children as a form of therapy. The camel was a

*Gil Riegler, milking a
camel for all it's worth.*
Photo: Nancy Kobert.

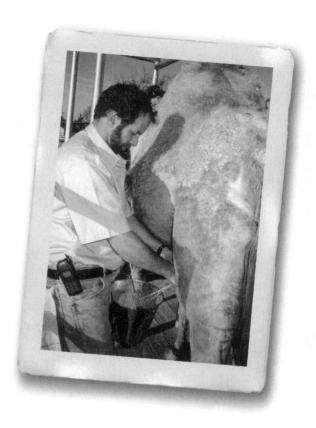

big hit with the kids and made a lasting impression on Riegler,
too. "I just fell in love with that camel," he says, quite
unabashedly. "I looked into his eyes and knew that this was
something I was going to do with the rest of my life."

So Riegler, with his fiancée, Nancy Kobert, purchased a
ranch in Ramona and began raising a camel herd with the ulti-
mate goal of establishing what has to be the country's only
camel dairy. They're still awaiting federal approval to begin dis-
pensing camel milk for consumption. In the meantime their
Oasis Camel Dairy markets camel-milk soaps, which Riegler
touts as being beneficial for skin care. He also takes the camels

around for demonstrations at local fairs and festivals, explaining the tricky art of getting milk from a camel.

"It's a lot different than milking a cow," he says. For one, camels drop their milk for only about ninety seconds, so you have to milk fast. And camels need a baby around to stimulate them to produce milk. All of which makes you wonder if it's all worth the effort. "Of course it is," Riegler says, asserting that camel's milk has potent curative powers and is essential to maintaining good health.

For more information visit the Web site at www.cameldairy.com or call (760) 787–0983.

A HOUSE WITH A SPIRITED HISTORY
San Diego

If you lived in San Diego in the 1880s and traveled in the right circles, you might have received an invitation for a most unusual evening of musical entertainment at the Villa Montezuma. The house was owned by Jesse Shepard, an opera singer who insisted that his musical talents were not learned by study, but intuitive, and that sometimes when he sang or played the piano, the spirits of famous composers actually played through him. Some evenings he would communicate with spirits of the afterlife, perhaps reenacting ancient Egyptian battle scenes or reaching such composers as Beethoven and Mozart.

Shepard had toured Europe and enchanted the Czar of Russia, the English Prince of Wales, and other notables before settling in San Diego in 1886. Benefactors built him a glorious Victorian mansion with a special salon with magnificent stained-glass windows for his musical entertainments.

Shepard was known for performing in low light, generating a decidedly mysterious atmosphere.

One spooky place.

Shepard stayed only a couple of years at the house. Subsequent owners had trouble holding onto the property, and through the years the house developed a reputation as being haunted. There were rumors of mysterious moans from a butler who had hanged himself from a cupola, ghastly figures in mirrors, and spooky beings wandering about. The mansion's foreboding Victorian design, with creepy gargoyles at some corners, only adds to its spine-chilling reputation. In addition to a historical landmark that points to a boom period in San Diego's history, Villa Montezuma stands as one of the most famous haunted houses in the world.

At present Villa Montezuma is open to the public as a museum operated by the San Diego Historical Society. It's also available for rental for weddings, if you dare. The house is located at 1925 K Street; (619) 239–2211.

A GHOSTLY TRADITION THAT'S HARD TO SWALLOW

San Juan Capistrano is known for the charming tradition of the swallows that return each year to nest in the town's old stone church. But smiling tourists celebrating the sweet ritual of homecoming tiny birds may be chilled to discover that this seemingly quaint town is also known for attracting a flock of ghosts with more sinister intentions. Ghost watchers maintain that there may be more ghoulish activity in San Juan Capistrano than in any other spot in the country. It's hard to find a historic building or site here that doesn't have some sort of ghost tale associated with it.

You can start with the old cemetery, the site of many poltergeist happenings. Then there's the El Adobe de Capistrano Restaurant, whose wine cellar used to be the city jail. Waiters who descend looking for a bottle of spirits sometimes have the feeling that unbottled spirits are watching them. And the ghost of a headless monk has been spotted loitering outside the restaurant, apparently without a reservation.

The town's many historical residences, some dating back to the late eighteenth century, may have their original inhabitants still lurking around. At the Montanez Adobe, for instance, people have detected a ghostly ball of light in the living room. The Rios Adobe, which has the distinction of being the oldest single-family home continuously occupied by the same family, also has its share of paranormal activity. Most often people have heard phantom boot steps in the house. Along the street there are stories of the White Lady of Capistrano wandering about, sometimes with a ghostly entourage.

So the next time you visit San Juan Capistrano, after noting the birds in the sky, keep a watchful eye for any haunted apparitions below.

THE CLOCK THAT GRIEVED
San Diego

The landmark Jessop's Clock, located outside the Horton Plaza shopping center, has kept incredibly accurate time since it was built in 1907. The massive timepiece, with a fifty-five-pound pendulum, has twenty dials, twelve of which tell time from various international locales. But did the clock with a worldly sense of time once display a sense of grief? That's the legend anyway, which stems from the special relationship between the clock and its maker.

This clock needed time to mourn its maker.

In the early 1900s Joseph Jessop envisioned a major clock that would sit outside his jewelry store and be a town centerpiece. He hired Claude Ledger to build it, and right away Ledger was a man obsessed. He had little time for anything but the clock. It took him more than a year to build, but it was worth the effort. When finished in 1907, the clock was exhibited at the state fair in Sacramento and won a first-place prize. It also picked up an unintentional souvenir: a tiny, carved brown bear placed on a swinging pendulum by a boy who wanted to give his toy a ride. It proved impossible to remove, and it remains on the clock to this day.

After the clock was built, Ledger continued to be fanatical about it, forbidding anyone to tinker with it or set its movement. Only two things temporarily stopped his precious clock from ticking: an earthquake and a horse-carriage accident that smashed the clock's base.

And then, on the day Ledger died, the clock mysteriously stopped. Some reports even say that it stopped again three days later on the day of Ledger's funeral. The strange occurrence made national headlines and was recorded in *Ripley's Believe It or Not*. Ledger's timepiece has thus earned the nickname as "The Clock That Grieved."

WYATT EARP, MAN OF SAN DIEGO
San Diego

Mention the name Wyatt Earp and you're likely to think of such dusty and lawless locales as Dodge City, Kansas, where he served as deputy marshal, or Tombstone, Arizona, where he was a gun-toting participant in the shootout at the OK Corral, settling a feud with the Clanton Gang in 1881. It would take a true historian to know that Earp spent a good

Ken Cilch keeps Wyatt Earp's San Diego history alive.

deal of his life in beachy San Diego, which in the late 1800s had a rough-and-tumble section of town that made Earp feel right at home.

Earp arrived in San Diego around 1885 with his third wife, Josie, and honed in on the city's infamous Stingaree District, where gambling, prostitution, theft, and murder were the norm. The Stingaree neighborhood was named after the fierce stingray fish in the San Diego Bay because it was said you could get stung worse in the district by its various vices and criminal activity.

When Earp arrived, San Diego was in the midst of a real-estate boom related to the gold rush in the hills of Julian. He invested heavily in property and also leased saloons and gambling halls. Within a few years the Stingaree district had more than one hundred bordellos and seventy saloons with such colorful names as Old Tub of Blood and First and Last Chance.

Earp left San Diego sometime before the turn of the century and a few years before citizen groups pressured the police to clean up the Stingaree area and put an end to the red-light district.

At present, thanks to urban renewal, the infamous Stingaree area has been transformed into the popular entertainment zone known as the Gaslamp Quarter, where the only place you're apt to get stung is in the wallet.

To recapture some of this history, you can stroll through the quarter and visit the Wyatt Earp Museum, housed inside Gaslamp Books. The museum features one of Earp's guns and a badge as well as many historical photographs and some mining artifacts.

The bookstore is located at 413 Market Street and can be reached at (619) 237–1492. A Web site is at www.wyattearp museum.com.

FEET OF BIBLICAL PROPORTIONS
San Diego

Walking on water may be miraculous to some, but it's pure science to participants in the annual Walk on Water competition at the University of San Diego.

Each year the school's engineering department invites students from local colleges and high schools to design shoes that will allow someone to do the seemingly impossible: walk across

A walk on the wet side. Photo: Leonard Perry.

the university's pool without falling in. It's not faith that gets the job done here but a good understanding of the principles of buoyancy, stability, and propulsion.

Teams of three or four enter the contest, with one person designated as the "shoe pilot." Making shoes out of surfboards or boat parts is considered cheating. Originality counts, but you can't spend more than $100 to make the miracle pair. These are really big shoes to fill, and successful teams make them out of material such as cardboard cylinders, fiberglass, or Styrofoam. Teams that miscalculate find out soon enough if their shoe computations were all wet.

Winners who successfully navigate the slalom course in the fastest times are, of course, decidedly buoyant.

For information about the next Walk on Water event, visit the Web site www.sandiego.edu/usdengr and click on the link to the event.

As Their World Turns
San Diego

If Al and Janet Johnstone feel as if their lives are going around in circles, you can't blame them. Not only is their house round, it literally spins. The views from the couple's 8,500-square-foot home atop Mount Helix are constantly changing, which is the whole idea.

Rotating buildings are unusual to begin with and are typically limited to novelty restaurants in tourist locales. That makes this pirouetting pad all the more unique.

When they were designing the house, the Johnstones pondered which room would have the best views. They decided that every room should. Indeed, why not? They can go to bed with the sunset and wake up with the sunrise without ever leaving the bedroom. Thanks to a specially designed swivel in the middle of the house, they were able to make sure that when the house turned, so did its electrical wiring and plumbing.

In another unique twist to home design, the garage has turntables that rotate their cars 180 degrees after parking so that the couple never has to back out of the driveway. The house also features a recreation room with a movable wall so that it can be resized, depending on how they want to use it that day.

Don't like the view? Just wait a minute.
Photo: Courtesy of Al Johnstone.

Depending on how fast they want to see the world turn, the Johnstones can regulate the home's rotation speed. At its slowest it does a full spin in a day. At full speed one rotation takes half an hour.

One thing they don't have to worry about is their world spinning out of control. The weight of the house ensures that. For more information take a spin over to www.rotatinghome.com.

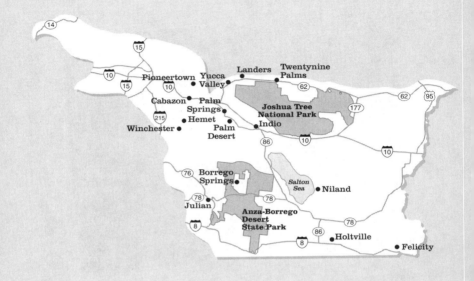

PALM SPRINGS AREA
AND SOUTHERN DESERT
REGION

Palm Springs Area and Southern Desert Region

A PROMISE TO TELL LIES, AND NOTHING BUT LIES
Borrego Springs

The truth about Thomas "Pegleg" Smith is that he was one heck of a liar. In saloons, on dusty trails, and around campfires all over the west in the mid-nineteenth century, Smith regaled folks with the story of a pure gold strike he had discovered somewhere in the desert. If only he could find it.

Smith was a silver-tongued devil when it came to talk of gold. He was also a horse thief who lost a leg when he amputated it himself after being hit by an Indian arrow. Or maybe not.

Out west, spinners of good yarns earn respect, and such is the case with Pegleg. Although he never did find his pot of gold, he has been honored in modern times with an annual liar's contest that bears his name. The contest is held on the first Saturday of April around a campfire near Borrego Springs.

The unique tribute to Pegleg is courtesy of Hollywood-set-designer Harry Oliver, who was so enamored of Pegleg's colorful story that he called himself "an agent for Pegleg's ghost." Oliver set up a monument to Pegleg in the Anza Borrego Desert, a sign that reads: LET THOSE WHO SEEK PEGLEG'S GOLD ADD TEN ROCKS TO THIS PILE. Now a 6-foot-high mound of stones stands piled behind the monument. Contestants have also been piling on tall tales at this site since the 1930s, when Oliver first organized a liar's contest there as a tribute to Pegleg.

Though Oliver's contest stopped in the late 1950s, it was resurrected in 1975 by a new group of Pegleg fans. Contestants are given five minutes to deliver a fanciful tale, which must involve Pegleg and gold, and to woo a crowd seated in lawn chairs around a roaring campfire. One year a storyteller told how Pegleg used a penguin as a compass; another described Pegleg's travel companion as a burrowing rhino with gold toenails.

Winners receive cast-off trophies collected from local thrift stores and recognition as the biggest liar in town. Contact the Borrego Springs Chamber of Commerce at (800) 559–5524 or visit the Web site at www.borregosprings.com.

JURASSIC PARKING LOT
Cabazon

Artist Claude Bell harbored a lifelong dream to create a work that was big and permanent. The realization of Bell's vision stuns travelers along an otherwise desolate stretch of freeway outside Palm Springs. What looms on the desert landscape are two giant concrete dinosaurs: a four-story tall, 150-foot-long brontosaurus and a 65-foot-high *Tyrannosaurus rex*. The brontosaurus appears to frown upon passing motorists, whereas the *T. rex* flashes a toothy glare.

Bell, a portrait artist for Knott's Berry Farm, began his project while in his seventies after buying about seventy-five acres in the tiny town of Cabazon. It took him eleven years and $250,000 to finish the brontosaurus in 1974, naming it Dinny. Thinking Dinny might be lonely, Bell began the T. rex a few years later and was almost done when, in 1988, he died. A slide

Who says dinosaurs are extinct?

planned for its backside and a viewing area in its head were never finished.

Bell had originally planned a cocktail lounge and restaurant for inside Dinny's belly, but he settled on a gift shop, still open to the public. Climb inside and you can peruse various dinosaur-themed toys, souvenirs, and books as well as experience the thrill of shopping inside the belly of a beast.

The dinosaur figures are off Interstate 10 in Cabazon. Call (706) 251–4800 for information.

In the Middle of Everything
Felicity

Jacques Andre Istel always dreamed of giving birth to a city. It's just that when the Frenchman envisioned his bustling metropolis in a barren desert terrain in the shadow of the Chocolate Mountains, many people saw his aspiration as a bit quixotic.

In 1959 Istel purchased 2,800 acres of land that boasted wind-spun columns of dust and little else. But Istel's dream lingered. First he fulfilled other pursuits, such as setting a world parachuting record in 1961 and helping to launch sport parachuting. But his city visions persisted. "The idea of starting a town in my old age was appealing," he says.

Istel launched a campaign to put his new city on the map even before it was incorporated. He had written a children's book about a dragon's quest to find the center of the world, so he extended his fairy tale to his real city and proclaimed it the center of the world. In 1985 he charmed the Imperial County Board of Supervisors into making his declaration official. The board passed a resolution designating a parcel of his future city as the true center of the universe. The following year the board approved the town of Felicity, which Istel named after his wife, Felicia.

Ever since that day, the bubbly Istel has been greeting visitors to the town with an exuberant cry of "Welcome to the Center of the World!" It's a claim that has also been supported by the Institut Géographique of France.

The world's core doesn't yet have a lot going on. Though Istel was adept at establishing the town as the world's mythical center, he has been less savvy with laying out the town's grid. "I realized that I'm not a developer," Istel admits.

Felicity does have a pink marble pyramid that marks the spot of the world's middle. Visitors also encounter the Stairway to Heaven, a 25-foot section of the original spiral staircase from the Eiffel Tower. There's also a general store, a post office, and even a California Highway Patrol headquarters.

Another curiosity at the site is a massive sundial, which features a three-dimensional bronze cast of Michelangelo's Arm of God, after the painting on the ceiling of the Sistine Chapel. The arm points toward a hill, where there are plans for a future church. Slowly, the center of the world is taking shape.

PLAY ON, RAMONA . . . AND ON AND ON
Hemet

When writer Helen Hunt Jackson witnessed the poor treatment of American Indians during a trip west in 1881, she was determined to write a book that would move people's hearts. Maybe Jackson was too good a writer, however. *Ramona,* her novel of 1884, became a best-seller all right, but most people ignored its message of social reform for American Indians and instead became swept up by the book's romantic tale of doomed lovers Alessandro and Ramona.

The book's popularity ignited a tourist boom to the San Jacinto area as faithful *Ramona* readers made pilgrimages to key locations mentioned in the book. Although her story was fiction, Jackson's novel mentions real places and plays up actual events. For instance, Alessandro's murder is based on the killing of American Indian Juan Diego, who was shot dead by a San Jacinto wagon driver in 1883. The wagon driver was never jailed for the offense. Savvy to the book's draw, Hemet officials staged a play version of the novel in 1923, enlisting the help of

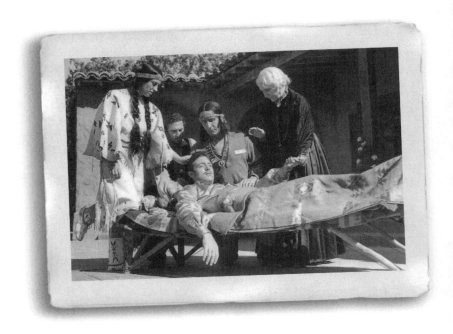

A 1930s production of Ramona, *the oldest outdoor drama in the United States.*
Photo: Courtesy of *Ramona* outdoor play, Hemet, California.

American dramatist Garnet Holme. He wrote the *Ramona* stage version and mounted the first production outdoors, using volunteers from the local community, and it has been that way ever since. The *Ramona* production is the oldest outdoor drama in the United States as well as California's official state play.

When the play was first staged, there were no seats for the audience. Now the Ramona Bowl amphitheater has seating for more than 6,600, but still there is no stage—the action takes place on sets on the hillside and in the canyon. Each year almost 400 local volunteers organize the show, and another 400 perform as actors, singers, dancers, and horsemen. Only the leads are paid, and in the past they have included some actresses who got their start on the Ramona stage, including Raquel Welch in 1959 and Anne Archer ten years later.

For ticket information call (800) 645–4465 or (909) 658–3111 or visit the Web site at www.ramonapageant.com.

A Town Celebrates Its Roots
Holtville

Most of us would consider it a stretch to think of carrots as cause for celebration. But Holtville, the self-proclaimed carrot capital of the world, has been hosting a Carrot Festival since 1948. The annual tribute to the crunchy root vegetable is fitting in these parts, as the Imperial Valley region prides itself on being the country's winter salad bowl. Thousands of acres here are set aside for carrot cultivation. The area's soft soil is apparently ideal for the carrot, and as much as 90 percent of the carrots consumed in the United States are grown here. That alone is enough to make anyone tilt a glass of carrot juice in merriment.

If you're looking for creative ways to prepare this nutritional food, the festival is a must. Recipe contests have yielded a flavorful bunch of carrot-infused dishes, including salsa, chutney, pasta, and even ice cream. To top it off, there's a carrot-themed parade and an arts-and-crafts display.

For dates of the annual festival, go to the Holtville Chamber of Commerce's Web site at www.holtvillechamber.ca.gov or call (760) 356–2923.

LOOKING FOR A DATE? THIS IS THE PLACE
Indio

When a festival features Arabian touches such as camel races and workers outfitted in veils and fezzes but also offers basic American staples such as corn dogs, monster-truck competitions and livestock shows, it becomes one strange blend of cultures enclosed on the same fairgrounds. That's the National Date Festival, held each February to celebrate the local date industry.

Though the fruit of the palm has been cultivated for more than 5,000 years in Arabia, it was introduced to the United States only at the beginning of the 1900s. After a few unsuccessful tries, dates eventually caught on in the Coachella Valley, which now produces about thirty-five million pounds of the sweet fruit each year, or more than 90 percent of the country's date production. The region's ties to the date industry are marked by the naming of towns with Arabian themes such as Oasis and Mecca and main thoroughfares such as Arabia Street in Indio.

A date festival began in 1921 in a small park and moved to the larger fairgrounds in Indio in 1947, where it has been a major tourist draw ever since. Each year more than 350,000 visitors drop by during the ten-day period for a wide range of entertainment, including hotly contested races that feature ostriches and camels ridden by jockeys. Other Arabian-themed events include the *Sands of Time,* a production of tales from the *Arabian Nights.*

There are plenty of chances to sample a variety of dates, including the region's staple, the Deglet Noor, and plenty of stands offering the always-popular date shakes. More than one hundred varieties of dates are grown here, and some connoisseurs sample and taste them with an intense scrutiny, assess-

Camel races are pretty popular at the National Date Festival.
Photo: Courtesy of Riverside County Fair and National Date Festival.

ing their texture and sugar content. If you've never had one, this is a great place for a first date. For more information visit www.datefest.org.

ROADSIDE APPEAL
Indio

If promoter P. T. Barnum's passion had been dates instead of circuses and museums, he probably would have turned into someone like Floyd Shields. After opening his date farm in

America's date-growing mecca, Shields knew he needed a gimmick to make his operation stand out. So in 1949 he built a 108-seat theater inside his date store and began offering visitors a special show. He lured them in from the highway with large signs proclaiming to unveil the secrets of *The Romance and Sex Life of the Date*.

In reality the show was an educational slide presentation, with narration by Shields, that explained how dates are grown and harvested.

The show's sensational title, much like one of Barnum's famous come-ons, promised more than it delivered. But visitors were made aware of date trivia such as how one male tree can fertilize forty-nine females. And visitors left with the sweet taste of dates in their mouths.

Shields, along with his wife, Bess, opened his first date store on Christmas Day in 1924. Because many Americans were unfamiliar with the fruit of the palm, some questioned why such a small wrinkled fruit was so expensive. Shields answered by escorting visitors out to his garden and explaining the difficult process of date cultivation. Then he came up with his legendary slide show in 1949 as a way of educating the public about dates—and drawing them into his store to make a purchase.

The theater still remains, and the story about the date's sex life is now offered in a video loop that runs all day. After the show visitors can sample dates as well as date crystals, a flat, dried version of dates produced from a process Shields patented years ago.

Shields Date Garden is located at 80-225 Highway 111 in Indio. Call (760) 347–0996 or visit them on the Web at www.shieldsdates.com.

Nuts about Screws
Julian

When Mel Kirsner retired from the fastener business in 1990, he couldn't bear to throw away the piles of catalogs and memorabilia he had accumulated in his four decades in the business. So he tucked the collection away for a few years and then added a third story to his house to display some of his historic wares. That was the beginning of Mell's Fastener Museum, which he eventually moved to a separate location in the hills of Julian.

Mel Kirsner is happiest among his nuts and bolts.

Photo: Judy Kirsner.

Judging by his collection, Kirsner is clearly a man fascinated by fasteners. On display are items such as bronze fasteners dating back to A.D. 3 in Rome, a box of carriage bolts from 1930, a fastener-salesman's travel case from 1920, and a massive bolt-and-nut cabinet from 1886 made from oak. For kicks there are whimsical figurines made from nuts and bolts. Mel's favorite is the National Screw Robot Man, which he described as "a very little guy made out of fasteners."

Kirsner began in his family's fastener business in 1958 and eventually came to California in 1963 to open his own shop, Pell Mell Supply. He'd buy surplus from a variety of sources, sometimes purchasing company floor sweepings or directly from scrap dealers. Then he'd sort through and organize the fasteners, boxing them for sale. Kirsner notes a claim to fame is that he has "sorted more fasteners manually than any other living person." So far, no one has come forward to dispute the claim.

Kirsner is also a man who knows his fastener history, pointing out curiosities such as the fact that the screw was invented in the 1700s, whereas the screwdriver didn't come along until the 1800s. It's enough to make anyone nuts.

For information about the museum, call (760) 765–0596 or take a virtual tour at www.mellsfastenermuseum.org.

DESERT FLOWER POWER
Landers

In this desolate stretch of high desert, any sign of color on the landscape besides shades of brown is a rare sight indeed, which makes Gubler Orchids a true oasis. Step out of the hot, dusty air and into Gubler's climate-controlled greenhouse and you'll be greeted by a rainbow of colors. Aside from the fact

Gubler Orchids is a flower-friendly desert oasis.

that you'll feel as if you can breathe freely again, the treat here is rows and rows of beautiful orchids in a dazzling display of brilliant color and plant vitality.

More than one million orchids are housed here, with more than a thousand different varieties of the sometimes delicate plant that would feel more at home in a tropical rain forest than a harsh desert locale. But the staff here keeps things just the way the orchids like it—moist, with fresh water from underground wells showered over them daily, and plenty of indirect sunlight. The plants are treated grandly right from the start, as seeds are grown in mother jars with a special blend of fungal nourishment that includes pureed bananas, pineapple juice, and charcoal. Then they're transplanted into small pots filled with tree bark. Orchids normally grow their first bloom in about five years, but the long wait is worth it, as these flowers explode in radiant colors and patterns and sometimes bear a memorable fragrance.

Gubler is one of the country's largest distributors of orchids, and it promises to ship them anywhere in the world. It's more fun to visit, though, because everyone gets a free half-hour tour. The first weekend in October Gubler hosts an annual orchid festival, which includes music and classes. For more information call (800) 482-5377 or visit www.gublers.com. The store is located at 2200 Belfield Boulevard.

THEY TOLD HIM TO BUILD IT
Landers

In 1947 George Van Tassel quit his job as an aviation engineer in Los Angeles and came to the desert in pursuit of a more laid-back lifestyle. Instead, his world became anything but quiet when he was soon visited by extraterrestrials from Venus. The interplanetary travelers told him how to construct a domed fountain of youth. "Build it," they said, "and you will live an extra twenty-five years."

And build it he did, toiling for eighteen years to erect a geodesic wooden dome he called the Integratron in a location long a hotbed for UFO sightings. When he wasn't working on the dome, he was holding space conventions at nearby Giant Rock, raucous events that sometimes drew thousands.

Van Tassel claimed that the Integratron would generate electrostatic energy that would rejuvenate human cells. Unfortunately, he died suddenly in 1978 before completing the project. Mysteriously, directions for operating the machine disappeared

What not to do to a cholla cactus.

THEY'VE GOT YOU UNDER YOUR SKIN

*F*rom a safe distance cholla cacti look, well, cuddly. Their silvery bristles appear like soft brushes, and the temptation is great to reach out and touch them.

But petting a so-called "teddy bear" cholla is a painful mistake often made in the Pinto Basin desert region, where they're quite common. That's because what looks so inviting are actually tiny barbs that dive under the skin when they make contact and remain planted there. Hence the plant's other common nickname, the "jumping cholla."

Desert legend has it that cholla are infused with malevolent intent and actually go out of their way to stab people. Scientists dismiss this as just a painful illusion.

At Joshua Tree National Park, visitors can wander through the Cholla Cactus Garden and see these mysterious plants up close. This is one place where it pays to walk carefully, as the short trail through the garden is lined with cholla tantalizingly close to the pathway's edge. A step in the wrong direction and visitors can take home a smarting souvenir.

This building may hold the key to prolonging life—
if someone knew how it worked.

soon after, and so the building remains a monument to one man's outer-space visions and belief in weird science.

At present new owners offer tours of the site and also use an upstairs sound chamber for unique acoustic treatments they call sound baths. Visitors recline in a suspended hammock in the room's center while pure tones are played on quartz-crystal singing bowls. Owner Nancy Karl, who likens the treatment to "brain flossing," says that it's highly therapeutic. The owners also lease the building for special events, such as yoga retreats and even the recent filming of a music video. Karl says that they're still hoping to unlock the mystery of the Integratron's cell-rejuvenation powers.

Call (760) 364–3126 for more information or visit www.inte gratron.com. The building is located at 2477 Belfield Boulevard.

The world's largest boulder—until a piece broke off.

A ROCK AND A SHARD PLACE

*F*or a natural wonder that has hosted many eccentric gatherings through the years, a stupendous stone, which locals claim is the world's largest boulder, goes by an ordinary name: Giant Rock.

For Native Americans this colossal rock was a deeply spiritual place where they held sacred ceremonies. During the 1950s and through the 1970s, it was the site of many space conventions held by UFO-believer George Van Tassel, who enthralled crowds in the thousands by channeling aliens. For a time he also lived with his family in a special chamber under the rock.

Giant Rock is located about a dozen miles north of Yucca Valley in a remote desert spot. It's seven stories high and 5,800 square feet in size, making it giant indeed. In 2001, however, a large chunk broke off, exposing a white granite interior and threatening its status as the world's top rock. Some blame the accident on repeated fires set beneath it, whereas others say the rock's demise was due to an earthquake. Graffiti taggers have since defaced the rock, and it's now a hangout for dune-buggy enthusiasts who cruise the area, a mere shell of its once-mighty past.

TELLING IT ON A MOUNTAIN
Niland

Leonard Knight had a dream of flying a big hot-air balloon painted with the words: GOD IS LOVE. He spent months sowing remnants together and crafting his own makeshift craft. It was 200 feet long and weighed more than 600 pounds, big enough for what he envisioned. But it wouldn't fly. Discouraged, Knight ended up in the desert near the Salton Sea and vowed to create his giant prayer to God by painting the side of a mountain.

What he couldn't achieve with his balloon Knight has certainly accomplished with his worshipful hill. Knight has created a brightly colored tribute to his love of God using latex paint. One section proclaims GOD IS LOVE in bright red-and-pink letters suspended over a large red heart, a message visible for miles. The rest of the mountain streams primary colors and assorted designs, including flowers, birds, nature scenes, and biblical writing, including the text of John 3:16 marked with more than 1,000 marbles.

Knight figures that his Salvation Mountain is coated with more than 100,000 gallons of paint. That got the attention of Imperial County officials. They were worried that he had created an environmental disaster, and they had plans to cart away the mountain and bury it in a toxic-waste dump.

But folks came to Knight's aid, and tests were done to determine that no lead contamination was taking place. The controversy brought free publicity. Suddenly curious tourists and folk-art researchers started dropping by. Knight's mountain has been featured in international art magazines, and he has been pictured on the cover of two art books and been the subject of television documentaries. Knight, who sometimes paints by moonlight and mostly lives off Social Security, remains humble, telling people: "I let my mountain do my talking." At three stories high his message is getting through.

A PARADE THAT'S WELL ABOVE PAR
Palm Desert

Maybe it was the searing desert heat that led residents here to launch a zany idea for a golf-cart parade back in the summer of 1964. Then again, when you live in a region with one of the highest concentrations of golf courses in the country (111 total), you're bound to think of something creative to do with all those carts.

Somewhere under that train engine is a golf cart.

Photo: Phil Cordova.

They called it Summer Madness when the first procession of decorated golf carts went putt-putt along El Paseo Drive. The scorching summer heat wilted some enthusiasm for this mad-cap parade, so it was moved to the fall, when temperatures are more likely to drop below 100 degrees.

Like most parades this one has annual themes, marching bands, drill teams, and celebrity marshals. But unlike any other parade, the focus here is on the elaborately decorated and battery-powered golf carts. Designers have gotten so creative in recent years that it's hard to tell where the golf cart ends and the parade float begins. Observers have described it as the Rose Parade in miniature. There are floats that look like planes, trains, animals, wedding cakes, giant beds, and other assorted inspired designs—in all, a golf-cart parade that really swings.

For dates for the annual Golf Cart Parade, contact the Palm Desert Chamber of Commerce at (760) 346–6111 or visit the Web site at www.golfcartparade.com.

A LIVE AND K ICKING
Palm Springs

When the Palm Springs City Council asked Riff Markowitz to organize a show at the Plaza Theatre, it was hoping he could help invigorate the landmark venue that formerly hosted radio shows by old-time entertainers Bob Hope and Jack Benny. Markowitz not only launched a production that revitalized the theater, he also pumped new life into the careers of former chorus girls.

The *Palm Springs Follies* is a vaudeville-revival show that features performers whose entertainment careers began in the Vaudeville era. The *Follies* cast is recognized by *Guinness Book of World Records* as the world's oldest professional chorus line.

WARNING: BARE CROSSING

New York has its Brooklyn Bridge, San Francisco its Golden Gate, and Venice, Italy, boasts the Bridge of Sighs. You can add to the list of famous crossings Palm Springs' Bridge of Thighs.

That's what they're affectionately calling a pedestrian bridge that spans the city's busy Indian Canyon Drive. It has been hailed as the world's first nudist bridge, as it connects two sides of a popular nudist resort. The walkway overpass was constructed so that guests of the resort could make the clothing-optional trek from one side of the street to the other without being spotted by members of the clothed world below. The overhead passageway is shrouded in beige-and-green sailcloth panels, so there's no peeking. The panels are double-layered, because builders realized that with one layer it was possible to detect shadow outlines of figures passing overhead.

Bridge designers are also hoping that inquisitive onlookers keep their eyes focused on the bridge's architectural flourishes on the outside—metal mesh wings stretching from its sides—rather than trying to envision the parade of flesh within.

Judy Bell, a high-kicking member of the world's oldest professional chorus line. Photo: Ned Redway.

Performers range in age from fifty-nine to eighty-nine. Many are grandmothers, having senior moments under the glare of floodlights amid sequins and slapstick routines.

When Markowitz first launched the show, a local scribe wryly asked him who would want to look at old ladies' legs. The answer is plenty of folks. The show has been a smash hit, seen by more than two million people since it opened in 1991.

When many of their peers might consider it a challenge just to get out of bed, these "Long-legged Lovelies" are kicking up a storm in dazzling and exhaustive three-hour performances, ten times a week during a season that runs from November through May.

When observers question that Markowitz is working his cast too hard, he answers that his elder performers are an inspiration to others. "It's more than just show business," he says, it's a "statement of hope that life goes on."

You can call the Palm Springs box office at (760) 327–0225 for ticket information or visit the *Follies* Web site at www.palmspringsfollies.com.

A TOUR THAT BLOWS PEOPLE AWAY
Palm Springs

When you think windmills, you're apt to conjure up a quaint image of a wooden device churning pleasantly in a pastoral Dutch setting. Early windmills were used to harness wind power to grind grain, hence the term "mill."

The modern windmill is anything but quaint. The more appropriate expression is "wind turbine," as these massive structures weigh thousands of pounds and have giant rotors that complete sweeps of half a football field in length.

A lot of hot air blows through these parts.

California produces 80 percent of the world's wind-generated electric power, and most of the machines doing the work are located near Palm Springs in an area dubbed by the U.S. Weather Service as the "Finest Natural Wind Tunnel in the World." Wind comes roaring through the San Gorgonio Pass, where wind-energy companies have staked out the future of wind power. Hundreds of massive white windmills that soar 150 feet into the air dot the landscape here like giant whirling dance lines. The area is so dependable when it comes to wind that every new windmill that has been developed for use in America has first been tested here.

So many travelers were stopping to take pictures of the windmills that Wintec, the company that operates many of the wind turbines, decided to offer a tour. Visitors are escorted through a forest of windmills in electric golf carts. For information about the tours, call (760) 251–1997 or visit the Web site at www.windmilltours.com.

By the Light of the Moon
Palm Springs

On the first day that Scott Scott ("Just call me Scott squared") moved to the desert in the mid-1980s, he found a trail and began hiking, and he's been hiking ever since. "I love the peace and solitude and the open expansive feeling of the desert, probably as much I love the mountains here," he says.

At least once a week, he blows up a strenuous trail that goes from downtown Palm Springs to the top of the city's tram ride. That's a distance of 11 miles and an elevation climb of 8,000 feet, a walk that Scott completes in about four hours. You should think twice if he asks you to come along.

A more reasonable pace is offered during excursions from Scott's Trail Discovery and Desert Safari company, which organizes guided treks, including a chance to explore the desert terrain by moonlight. A van shuttles hikers to a "magical spot" about forty-five minutes out of town before dusk on the night of a full moon. As night falls, hikers wander along a 5.5-mile tour of a barren landscape eerily lit by the moon.

"It's really spectacular. It makes the terrain look like a moonscape," Scott says. "Because you are not able to see as much, you're listening and sensing other stuff around you."

Hiking by moonlight is one way to beat the desert heat.
Photo: Courtesy Palm Springs Hiking.com.

Snacks and water are made available, as are flashlights, although the moon's radiance makes it possible to walk about without one.

The moonlight hikes do have one advantage over daylight treks: It's a lot cooler at night. Though daytime temperatures sometimes climb above 110 degrees during summer, they can drop to a more manageable 80 degrees at night.

For the more adventurous, Scott's company sometimes offers a nude hike by moonlight, organized in conjunction with a local nudist resort. "People find that to be a really freeing experience," he says. The Full Monty excursion allows hikers the rare opportunity to moon the moon.

For more information call (760) 770–9191 or (888) TO–SAFARI or visit the Web site at www.desertsafari.com.

MOVING INTO A VACUUM
Pioneertown

Pioneertown has all the outward signs of a real town, including a bank, a restaurant, a motel, a bowling alley, and a main street—even residents. But Pioneertown is one of the most unusual communities in the country, for it was never intended to be a real place at all.

Instead, Pioneertown was constructed in 1946 to be the faux backdrop for dozens of westerns that were shot here, including the popular films of Gene Autry and Roy Rogers. Walking down its main street, you'll feel yourself either transported back in time or as if you're heading for a celluloid showdown at high noon.

Though the town included western facades to give it an authentic old-time look for filming, it also featured real amenities like lodgings and a restaurant so that film crews would

There may be more bowling pins than people in Pioneertown.

feel more comfortable while working on location. Once the movie crews moved out, real people moved in, creating a small community amid the movie scenery that still persists. From April through November some locals stage shootouts along Main Street to thrill visitors.

One enduring attraction here is Pioneer Bowl, opened in 1947 with Roy Rogers throwing out the first ball—rumored to be a strike, of course. At present, except for the addition of automatic pinsetters, it still operates just as it did during filming days.

To learn more about the town, visit its Web site at www.pioneertown.com.

WHO LEFT THE LIGHTS ON?

*S*trange sightings in the desert are nothing new. Tales of ghosts, UFOs, odd phenomena, and other unexplained experiences have long been reported in the region that is now known as Anza Borrego Desert Park.

One reported sighting here has spooked travelers for decades: the periodic and mysterious appearance of peculiar "ghost lights," or eerie fireballs, that illuminate the slopes of Oriflamme Mountain. Miners in the late 1800s reported "burning balls" that sometimes appeared as fireworks on Oriflamme, which means golden flame. Others talked about a "spirit light" that looked as if it was moving up and down along a creek.

Researchers say the first known sighting was by a stagecoach driver in 1858. Others followed, all describing pretty much the same thing: balls of fire that appeared to climb into the air and then explode.

Some people dismissed the lights as signals from bootleggers who were hiding in the hills. Scientists explain that they could be caused by desert winds blowing against quartz deposits, creating sparks. Another less scientific theory is that they are "money lights" to mark deposits of buried treasure or gold. Those trying to solve the mystery of strange night lights here are still in the dark.

MEN WILL BE BOYS
Pioneertown

A lot of kids grow up playing cowboys and Indians. Then there are those who grow up and still play cowboys and Indians.

Take Ernie Kester, or "Doc," as he's come to be known. He lives in Pioneertown, the site of filming a few decades ago of many notable television and movie westerns, the kind of action dramas that Kester grew up watching and dreaming about.

Now Kester lives out his western fantasy along with the dozen or so other permanent residents of Pioneertown. Kester runs the Pioneertown Motel, right off the town's main drag. On most weekends you'll find Doc strapping on his boots and holstering up his Colt pistol and heading out to hunt down the bad guys in town. And sometimes Doc is the villain who gets his due from the armed badges in town.

This fantasy is all part of a western reenactment group that Kester founded a few years ago to cater to Pioneertown tourists. The group, known as the Pioneertown Posse, stages elaborate shootouts in the heart of this western city. As the crowd looks on, sometimes as many as a dozen or so players are gunned down in a flurry of fake bullets.

Kester says he got the nickname "Doc" during one of the group's first skits, when he played a doctor who hunts down a greedy land baron. "The name stuck after that," he says.

Visitors who stay at Doc's hotel will get more than just a room; they'll get an extensive history of all the westerns shot in town. A word of advice: If Doc says checkout is at high noon, you'd better be ready to clear out.

The Pioneertown Motel can be reached by calling (760) 365–4879.

THE SEA THAT WAS NEVER MEANT TO BE

*F*irst of all, the Salton Sea is not really a sea. It's a lake. And a pretty big one. It's the largest inland body of water in California, more than twice the size of Lake Tahoe, and it measures 35 miles in length and 15 miles across.

The Salton Sea is the result of a major goof by urban planners in the early 1900s, when engineers tried to temporarily divert water from the Colorado River. The river jumped the levee, however, and flooded a dry bed known as the Salton Sink. Evaporation was supposed to make the accidental lake disappear, but agricultural runoff has continually fed it, creating a vibrant ecosystem in the middle of the desert that is the world's largest stopover for migratory birds. Each February bird-watchers flock to the Salton Sea Bird Festival to admire the thousands of fowl gathered there.

The Salton Sea lives up to its name in that it's very salty; in fact, it's 25 percent more salty than the Pacific Ocean. And with no river feeding it, it's getting saltier each year, threatening the many fish stock that have thrived here, including the tilapia. If it gets much saltier, they'll die. Even now, algae blooms sometimes chock off oxygen in the water and kill large numbers of fish. More than eight million fish died on a single day a few years ago.

Developers at one time had big plans for the area, targeting Salton City as the next Palm Springs. The area enjoyed a glamour period during the 1960s, when thousands of boaters powered across the watery expanse at high speeds, as the sea's high salt content makes it the fastest water for boaters in the country. In the past, Salton City drew big names such as Rat Packers Frank Sinatra and Dean Martin and dignitaries such as President Eisenhower.

Now it's all gone, with only street names such as Desert Manor and Acapulco to remind visitors of the city's once-grand dreams. Some blame the decline on the sea's pungent aroma—compared to that of sulfur dioxide—or the sight of many dead fish that periodically litter its banks.

Many people worry about what will happen to the migratory birds if the sea becomes too salty to support the fish they feed on. Unless a solution is found, the lake that appeared as an oasis a century ago may be in for a dry future.

A DESERT BRIGHT LIGHT
Twentynine Palms

Noble Richardson grew up in the high-desert town of Twenty-nine Palms and eventually left to study art in Los Angeles, carving out a living as a painter and silk screener.

Noble Richardson creates one-of-a-kind lamps from cacti.

"It's hard to make a living in the fine-arts business," he acknowledges. It wasn't until he returned to town that he hit upon a money-making idea that merged his artistic skills with his desert roots.

The idea hit him, he recalls, when he was painting in the desert and noticed all the dead cactus wood lying all around. Remembering tourist souvenirs he used to see as a kid, Richardson decided to gather up the pieces of dead wood and make them into decorative lamps. Suddenly he had a hit.

Using dried trunks from fallen cholla and saguaro, and the occasional Joshua tree, Richardson fashions one-of-a-kind table and standing lamps made from cacti. He adds brass and copper accents and tops them off with shades of hammered copper or rawhide. In his studio off a dusty road just outside of the town's main drag, he used to churn out about 200 of the lamps a year, numbering each one as a unique and practical art piece.

In recent years he's slowed down his lamp production so that he can work more on photography and painting. But he welcomes visitors to his studio as long as they call ahead to make an appointment: (760) 367–2945.

M u r a l   M a n i a
Twentynine Palms

People interested in learning the history of Twentynine Palms don't have to pore over dusty archives; they can simply study what's on the town's walls. There they'll find massive murals that tell the town's rich history in a series of colorful documentary depictions, painted mostly on available blank walls of commercial buildings.

On the side of a thrift store along the town's main drag is a major wall painting that illustrates the history of Dirty Sock

If there's a spare wall in this town, it's probably covered with a historical mural.

Camp, a tribute to eager miners who sometimes used their hosiery to separate gold from mercury. On an outside wall of a Chinese restaurant, visitors can learn about historic floods that once caused major destruction in the town before a flood-control channel was erected in 1969.

A local arts council began the Oasis of Murals project in 1994. The council decides the subjects and then commissions the muralists. One work, which commemorates a long-standing boys basketball tournament, was painted by twenty-one artists in one day on the wall of a local handball court.

Another mural highlights a mythic figure in the town's past: Mural number 6 is dedicated to Jack Cones, known in these parts as "the Flying Constable." Cones, who was head lawman in town from 1932 until 1960, was known for patrolling his turf by flying at low altitudes in his Piper J-3 Cub. Truly a larger-than-life figure, that's how he's portrayed on a long wall along the side of a bookstore.

You can take a virtual tour of the Oasis of Murals at www.oasisofmurals.com or contact the council at (760) 361–2286.

Getting over the Training Hump
Winchester

If your pet dog is misbehaving, chances are there are dozens of trainers nearby who would offer to help. But if your pet camel turns into a spitting, stubborn beast, who can lend a hand in getting the humped animal to mind his manners? That would be Bill Rivers, a second-generation animal trainer who operates what is probably the only camel-training school in the country.

"An untrained camel can get real pushy sometimes," Rivers explains. "Camels are real easy to acquire. People don't need special permits for them. So they buy a camel and think they're real neat, but then they can't control them."

Rivers's camel-training workshops aren't meant as a quick fix. He says it takes about three years to train a camel, and it helps if you start when it's young. But his workshops offer tips on everything from giving camels praise to training them to "koosh," or sit down. Camels are fairly smart, Rivers explains, and with training they can pull carts, be ridden, and perform "different tricks."

Rivers grew up around animals because of his dad, who had a Wild West show and trained animals such as horses, buffalos, tigers, and camels. His dad had a friend who had an exotic-animal business, which intrigued Rivers, and he also had a beautiful daughter, who interested him even more. Eventually he married the man's daughter and got his training with exotic animals before starting out with his own animal ranch. He now trains about forty different animals—including steers, American buffalo, water buffalo, ostriches, and, of course, camels—and makes them available for movie roles. For one movie he had to train a camel to chase after a man and then put his foot on the man's chest. Training, he says, requires a mix of "time and common sense."

If you don't own a camel, Rivers offers camel rides and also makes his animals available for special events. For more information contact his Movieland Ranch at (909) 926–1194 or visit his Web site at www.movielandanimals.com.

SERMON ON THE YUCCA VALLEY MOUNT
Yucca Valley

When it came to sculpting religious figures, Antone Martin always thought big. His first religious figure was a 10-foot-tall, four-ton statue of Christ preaching the Sermon on the Mount. Martin thought it would be perfectly displayed at the rim of the Grand Canyon, but the National Park Service didn't agree. That's when a pastor from the high-desert town of Yucca Valley suggested an alternative—a 3.5-acre site on a small hill overlooking the town.

Martin was so enamored of the site that the aircraft worker from Inglewood moved to the desert town and spent the last years of his life there creating more than three dozen massive,

Two of Antone Martin's colossal religious statues.
These depict the Sermon on the Mount.

white concrete statues depicting biblical highlights from
Christ's life. When Martin died in 1961, the site was willed to
San Bernardino County, with the provision that it be kept open
as a free public park.

Now visitors can wander through the small hillside space
known as Desert Christ Park and contemplate the various
tableaus depicted by the oversize figures, including Christ
instructing the Twelve Apostles, prayers at Gethsemane, and a
125-ton slab portraying the Last Supper. A recent earthquake
damaged several of the figures, but a local foundation is raising money for restorations. The park is still free, and visitors
are encouraged to wander among the Joshua trees and white
figures in a setting that is eerily serene and spiritual. The park
is located at 26000 Sunny Slope Drive.

LIFE ON THE SLAB

As neighborhoods go, Slab City has a lot going for it: low crime, friendly neighbors, and wide-open spaces, for starters, not to mention free rent. Of course, to enjoy these amenities you have to have a certain grittiness and a suitable mobile home because all that's really here are tumbleweeds and concrete-slab foundations left over from a former World War II marine base.

Slab City is the unofficial name of an area of about 640 acres of state-owned land in the Mojave Desert near the town of Niland. It drew its first residents in the mid-1960s. Since then, it has become popular with hundreds of snowbirds from colder climates up north. They camp out here from October through April in all sorts of recreational vehicles to enjoy the warm weather and rent-free accommodations. The snowbirds are mostly retirees, and some are members of active singles groups. About one hundred more hardy souls live here year-round, scrounging for a living and enduring scorching summer temperatures.

The leftover concrete slabs get turned into patios, dance floors, and other creative uses, one of many ways residents here improvise their desert lifestyle. There's no utility service, so most residents use solar cells attached to the roofs of their RVs to power their necessities, including the main source of entertainment here: television. Water is stored in fifty-gallon tanks and purchased from nearby towns.

Slab City hostess Linda Barnett makes nightly announcements on a CB channel, letting slabbers know of vital services and events. The snowbirds make sure they make a generous donation to the Niland Fire Department each year so that the department looks out for them. Slab City residents rent post-office boxes in Niland year-round.

The Imperial County Sheriff's Department is officially the law here, but slabbers come here because there really isn't any law. Many come to escape all that, and it looks as though their desert oasis will last for some time. California has tried for years to sell the land, but no one seems willing to buy, a fact that's probably toasted here during daily happy hour, which starts around 3:00 P.M.

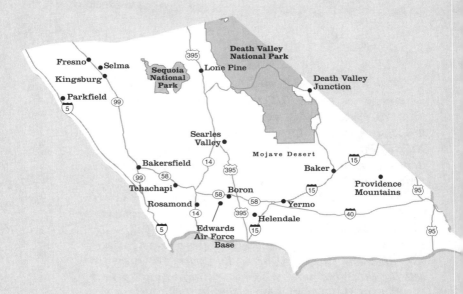

CENTRAL VALLEY, DESERTS, AND
SEQUOIA NATIONAL PARK

Central Valley, Deserts, and Sequoia National Park

Baker doesn't come by its name by accident. The desert gateway town literally bakes, especially in summer, when temperatures can soar to 120 degrees. Thousands of travelers using the town as a pit stop on their way to Las Vegas or Death Valley National Park often emerge from their refrigerated transports, step into the ovenlike air of Baker, and ask the obvious question: "Geez, how hot is it here?"

Will Herron, who owned the Bun Boy Restaurant and other commercial property in town, decided to erect a towering tribute to the day's temperature so that no one would have to guess. He built a colossal structure that easily became the world's tallest thermometer, dwarfing the previous record holder by more than 100 feet.

Baker's thermometer measures 134 feet tall, designed to commemorate the highest temperature ever recorded in North America, 134 degrees Fahrenheit set in nearby Furnace Creek in 1913.

When Herron announced his plans, some locals grumbled that it would be an eyesore, whereas others fretted that high winds might knock it down. In fact, a wind storm snapped the thermometer a few feet above its base a few days before its

It's hard to miss Baker's main attraction.
Photo: National Park Service.

scheduled dedication in 1991, sending the needle-shaped column of concrete and electronic lights crashing down.

That was only a temporary setback, however, as the thermometer rose again a short time later and now remains as a beacon to millions of travelers and a monumental reminder that the desert is sure one hot place.

The thermometer's hard to miss. You'll see it as you pass Baker on Interstate 15, located near the Bun Boy Restaurant at 72155 Baker Boulevard.

A MAGICIAN MOST FOWL
Bakersfield

Grant Schofield was born in 1933, the Chinese Year of the Rooster. Much later in his life he embraced the essence of his Chinese birth sign and clucked his way to fame.

After retiring from working as a parole officer and a juvenile-court referee, Schofield longed for a second career as a magician. He read how some performers used rubber chickens in their acts. Schofield decided to go one better and become a chicken himself.

He had special clown's shoes made that resembled chicken feet, and he adorned himself in feathery yellow attire with lots of fowl flourishes. He bought more than 200 books on chickens and incorporated various chicken props into his act, billing himself as the Great Granzini, or the Travelin' Chicken Man. Locals just refer to him as El Pollo Loco.

His PT Cruiser sports orange-and-yellow flames and features a waving chicken in the back window and one on the roof riding a surfboard. He calls it his chicken "coupe."

Schofield says he got the itch to perform while dealing with thousands of kids each year in juvenile court. He would some-

Grant Schofield is a chicken and proud of it.
Photo: Grant Schofield.

times perform magic acts for them or blow up balloons to keep them entertained and relaxed in court. "I didn't want them to feel that the court was a bad thing for them," he says.

Now he performs for kids professionally, telling groan-inducing chicken jokes and performing magic acts such as hiding coins inside eggs.

With his elaborately festooned vehicle and costume, Schofield is a hard guy to miss around town, and he loves the attention from passersby. His wife, however, is more reserved but takes her husband's new career in stride. She's often seen wearing a T-shirt that Schofield gave her that reads: MY NEXT HUSBAND WILL BE NORMAL.

For more information cross the street over to Schofield's Web site at www.granzini.com.

THE MACHO MULES
Boron

You don't often associate mules with terms like "dashing," "adventurous," and "swarthy." But one group of mules earned those accolades. Their brawny heroics, in fact, inspired a Hollywood movie, a corporate logo, and legions of fans. They were the fabled animals, known collectively as the Twenty-Mule Team, who hauled tons of borax through Death Valley in the 1880s, when no man or machine could get the job done.

Borax, referred to by prospectors as "white gold," was discovered near Furnace Creek Ranch, and a mining operation was started in 1881. But only the long mule trains, driven by rugged mule skinners, could get the finished product to Mojave's rail line, more than 160 miles way. The mules hauled the huge wagons, carrying more than thirty-seven tons of ore and water across the harsh terrain, an arduous journey that

The celebrated mules of the American West.
Photo: National Park Service.

took about sixteen days. Drivers controlled the mules with a jerk line that measured more than 120 feet.

The story of the mule team and its most famous driver, Borax Bill, is told in the Wallace Beery film, *20-Mule Team.*

In the town of Boron, which gets its name from the element contained in borax, there are two tributes to the mules and the white gold they hauled. There's the Twenty-Mule Team Museum, which has more than four rooms of artifacts and also offers a thirty-minute video on the town's famous element called *Boron: The Light Heavyweight.* Watch it and you can learn how borax can be processed and used for dozens of products, including soaps, medicines, and glass. Just a few miles out of town, the Borax Visitor Center offers several displays that tell the story of borax, including a large replica of one of the twenty-mule teams in action. The museum can be reached by calling (760) 762–7432. The Borax Center's phone is (760) 762–7588.

AFTER THE RACE HOW ABOUT A NICE REST ON A BED OF NAILS?
Death Valley

Just standing in the scorching heat of Death Valley would be enough of an endurance test for most people. That's why it's a bit hard to comprehend the Badwater UltraMarathon. You have to question the sanity of an elite group of distance runners who compete in what is one of the world's most grueling races. It begins in Badwater, the lowest locale in the Western Hemisphere, and ends with a partial climb up Mount Whitney, the tallest peak in the continental United States at 8,360 feet.

This crazy 135-mile race could be held in winter, when temperatures would be more comfortable, but that might give it some degree of sanity. Instead, it's held in the dead of summer, when race temperatures are usually a scorching 125 degrees.

The winning time is usually about twenty-five hours or so. In 2002 the winner, Pam Reed, reportedly stopped only once to check a blister and eat a peanut-butter sandwich. Some people take two days to crawl to the finish. What happens along the way to the seventy-five or so competitors is noteworthy. Feet swell. Gallons of sweat pour off them. As their bodies begin to break down, it's no longer a race but more like a hallucinatory trip. Runners have reported seeing dead people, flying saucers, mysterious herds of cows, even little men pulling sleds.

Scientists studying the limits of the human body eagerly follow the race to study the breakdown process, using the competition as their own field laboratory. The biggest question might be why anyone does it. There is no cash prize.

Not satisfied with completing the race once, some competitors have been known to hit the finish line, turn right around, and head back to the start, what's known as doing a "double." Of course, on the way back, it's all downhill.

DANCING UP A DESERT STORM
Death Valley Junction

A flat tire helped Marta Becket find her true calling. She had known since the age of three that she wanted to be a dancer and stage entertainer, and she had performed in New York City nightclubs and even on Broadway before creating a one-woman show and taking it on the road. In 1967, while on vacation from her tour, she and her husband got a flat tire and went to get it repaired in Death Valley Junction, a once-booming mining town that by the 1960s had more cats than people.

While waiting, Becket wandered to an abandoned social hall and peered through a door hole. Many people would have been discouraged by what she saw: A broken-down stage, a leaky roof, a warped floor, and a few benches were all that was left in the abandoned building. But to Becket it was pure desert gold. In that run-down place she saw her future. "The building seemed to be saying 'Take me . . . I offer you life,'" Becket explains on her Web site.

So she and her husband stayed, renting the hall for $45 a night. Becket created a one-woman dance-and-theater piece and performed her first show in 1968 to an audience of twelve. She has been doing it ever since, even though her husband eventually left. In the 1980s she incorporated stage-manager Thomas Willett into her act for comic relief. After each show she stays around to sign autographs and sell her paintings.

Becket is now approaching eighty, but the show goes on, even if no one shows up. After all, someone is always watching—the figures of kings and queens and nuns and angels that Becket spent six years painting on the theater's walls and ceiling of what is now called the Amargosa Opera House.

Becket now owns the town and also operates the hotel there as well. Call (760) 852–4441 or visit www.amargosaopera house.com for ticket information.

A Big Blast at the Park
Death Valley National Park

Visitors approaching Ubehebe Crater may simply be impressed by the size of this hole in the ground, which is 700 feet deep and more than half a mile across. Yup, that's one big hole. Even more astonishing, though, is the story of how it got there.

Ubehebe Crater is what's left after a volcano blew itself to bits.
Photo: National Park Service.

It happened not long ago, geologically speaking, maybe 3,000 or so years ago, give or take a few decades. The crater was at one time a volcano, and an active one at that. If you happened to be in the neighborhood back then, you would have witnessed one of nature's most remarkable and explosive displays. Red-hot magma gushed to the surface, surging through fault lines in the earth, meeting up with water-soaked rock. The magma superheated the water faster than a microwave defrosts a frozen dinner. This set off a steam-powered explosion that sent tons of rock soaring into the air at more than 100 miles per hour, leaving behind several impressive craters. The biggest one is called Ubehebe, a name given to it by Native Americans, who referred to it as the "basket in the rock."

Many visitors simply wander up to the crater's edge and stand in awe. Others hike into it, getting a geology lesson on the way down as they observe different layers of rock more than a million years in the making. Either way, the site prompts visitors to contemplate the big bang long ago, when a volcano blew itself into oblivion.

WHO NEEDS A GLOBAL POSITIONING SYSTEM WHEN YOU'VE GOT DANGLING TEAKETTLES?
Death Valley National Park

Finding your way around Death Valley can be tricky. Wide expanses of desert terrain offer little in the way of serviceable landmarks, so you take what you can get. And in the northern end of the park, that means looking out for a peculiar directional sign festooned with a wild assortment of teakettles: Teakettle Junction.

It's not a town; it's just a painted wooden sign offering a few helpful directional arrows to popular destinations to let tourists know they're headed the right way. It has become customary for travelers to hang old teakettles on the sign as they pass by, which makes some sense because the middle of the desert is hardly the place to be brewing up a pot of hot tea, so why not leave the kettle behind?

Terry Baldino, a park supervisor, thinks the tradition may have started years ago when one traveler left a kettle as a marker for friends who were coming by later. "It's become quite a tradition. It's pretty amazing," he says.

Some innovative visitors have expanded on the theme and

Where teakettles hang out to dry.
Photo: National Park Service.

strung up other items such as coffee mugs, pots and pans, or "anything that has something to do with holding water," Baldino says. So many items are suspended from the sign that park personnel routinely remove some so that the sign doesn't get too crowded with discarded housewares. The kettles change with the seasons.

The sign is certainly an intriguing photo opportunity for desert travelers, as much as other more legendary park sites. And it's comforting to know that once you've spotted the dangling kettles, you have an idea of your location.

The teakettle tradition has spawned a similar ritual at another park location with a different theme, Baldino says. This one is called Crankshaft Junction.

DIGGING A BIG HOLE FOR HIMSELF

As a bit of an eccentric loner, William Henry Schmidt wasn't unlike other gold prospectors who came to Last Chance Canyon near Copper Mountain in the early 1900s. His constant companions were his two pack animals, hence his nickname, "Burro" Schmidt.

In 1906, when he started digging a tunnel through Copper Mountain as a shortcut for bringing ore to rail lines, it made some sense. And then it didn't, because soon after he started his tunnel, a new road and rail line made his shortcut unnecessary. Schmidt kept digging anyway through the granite rock, using only picks, hammer, a hand-operated drill, and dynamite. He kept digging, for the next thirty-two years, until he finally broke through. Along the way he uncovered several potential veins of valuable ore, but he only had tunnel vision at this point, continuing on to daylight and not stopping for any prospecting.

Schmidt removed an estimated 2,460 cubic yards of rock, creating a tunnel 2,087 feet long. The tunnel, which was roomy at the start, became more cramped at the end, perhaps because Schmidt was eager to finish his task after all those years. He was sixty-seven years old when he stopped digging.

In the 1940s Ripley's Believe It or Not recognized his tunnel as "the greatest one-man mining achievement in history." A plaque at the tunnel entrance praises Schmidt for his "determination and perseverance." Later in life he earned a second nickname: "the Human Mole."

Schmidt died in 1954, but his burrowing feat endures. Each weekend a few dozen people trek to the site and stroll through his tunnel, ruminating in the darkened interior about one man's dogged achievement.

A ROCK-AND-ROLL MYSTERY
Death Valley National Park

There's nothing strange about strange sightings in Death Valley. See something odd here or there and you'll likely chalk it up to the heat playing tricks on your brain. One of the most puzzling visions here has to be the mysterious rolling rocks in a remote area aptly named the Racetrack.

The Racetrack is an oval-shaped, dry lake bed shadowed by a rock formation known as the Grandstand. Scattered across the clay surface of the lake are dozens of rocks. Fair enough. It's just that trailing the rocks are grooved tracks, as if the rocks had somehow been in motion across the lake bed. Some of the tracks are several hundred feet in length; some go in a straight line, whereas others curve and even loop. The problem is that no one has actually seen the rocks move.

This rock, and others, move in mysterious ways.
Photo: National Park Service.

THEY NAMED IT SKIDOO, AND THEN THEY SKEDADDLED

Skidoo wasn't a town for very long. It rose up in 1906, when gold was discovered, and that's about all the attraction a place needed back then to go from empty plains to full-blown town.

Within a year Skidoo boasted about 700 people and all the makings of a fine western gold camp, including the requisite bank, newspaper, saloon, and brothel. Skidoo even had the classic jaunty name, most likely tied to the length of the town's fabled water pipeline, which was 23 miles long. That number conjured up the era's famous slogan, "Twenty-three Skidoo."

No one knew at the time how prophetic that name would be. For a while the town prospered, but when the gold ran out, so did the people. That's another common history to the area's many ghost towns. By 1917 it was mostly over, and in 1922 only one Skidoo resident remained, a prospector named Old Tom Adams.

Nowadays you have to look hard for any trace that the town existed at all. The National Park Service felt obligated to put a sign there to mark the former civilization, centrally located in Death Valley National Park. Visitors won't find any remaining buildings—just rusted metal pieces on the ground and hundreds of mining tunnels and shaft remnants.

There are rumors that a ghost haunts this ghost town, the spirit of a man who killed the town's banker and then was lynched by enraged locals. Some people say they hear his voice, or maybe it's the wind blowing through the empty space that was once a town.

Scientists and casual observers have debated for decades what force might be responsible for the rocks' movement. It's Death Valley's version of crop circles.

Heady scientists have brought intricate equipment and complicated physics formulas to bear upon the mystery. The most likely cause, some suggest, is that the rocks slide across the lake bed propelled by strong winds. It helps if there has been a recent rain to slicken the clay surface.

To visitors without protractors and pocket protectors, the eerie rock movements are just another baffling piece of desert lore and beauty. Some have compared the track patterns to intricate dance movements, as if the rocks, when no one was looking, engaged in some kind of sensuous ballet for their own benefit. Better not to know why and just appreciate it for what it is: another desert oddity.

A GRAND DUPE AND HIS CASTLE
Death Valley National Park

In a region with plenty of eccentric characters and tellers of tall tales, Walter E. Scott is in a league all his own. His life story is one of Death Valley's most colorful legends. Born in 1872, he first earned fame as a stunt rider in Buffalo Bill Cody's Wild West Show. He even hauled borax with a mule rumored to have diamond-studded shoes.

Scott earned the nickname "Death Valley Scotty" and found his true calling mining gold. At least, that's what he told anyone within earshot when he frequented fine bars and hotels out west. He lured gullible investors into giving him money to help him mine his claims, ventures that apparently never panned out.

One of Scott's backers was Albert Johnson, a Chicago businessman who had made a fortune in the insurance industry.

*One of the desert's great hoaxes: Scotty's Castle, under construction
in the 1920s.* Photo: National Park Service.

He gave Scott thousands of dollars to mine a desert claim and
then traveled west to see the mine for himself. Surprisingly,
even when Johnson realized that Scott's claim of golden riches
was seriously overstated, Johnson wasn't angry. In fact, he
grew to like Scott, and the desert air, which improved his
health. So he built an ornate two-story villa with archways,
towers, and parapets—an oasis of splendor in the barren
desert—which was completed in 1927. Scotty told everyone the
massive residence was built with his gold-mining fortune, and
Johnson went along with the gag as the house became known
as Scotty's Castle.

A REPUTATION WELL EARNED

*C*rossing Death Valley was truly a life-or-death experience for one group of determined and unlucky travelers. The story of their ill-fated journey is how Death Valley got its lethal name.

A group of gold-seeking pioneers set out from Salt Lake City in October of 1849 bound for the West Coast, late in the year for such a trip. Only two years earlier the Donner Party had also made a tardy departure with disastrous consequences as they were trapped by storms in the Sierra Nevada. But this group, led by Jefferson Hunt, believed they knew of a shortcut to the West Coast that would save time and be safer to travel during winter. Mishaps followed, including the use of a bogus map and divisions of the group into smaller parties. One subgroup, led by the Reverend John Brier, would endure more than four months of arduous travel, which eventually brought them into what is now known as Death Valley. There they burned their wagons, killed ailing oxen for food, and walked the rest of the way to Los Angeles, which they didn't know was about 500 miles away.

They trudged onward until they finally made it through the valley of purgatory, offering as a parting a "goodbye to Death Valley." The story of these lost "49ers" is how the valley got its name, although historians now differ on how many people actually died along the way. Some say only one, an elderly gent, whereas others say about a dozen. If you'd like to relive this pioneer experience, just drive into the valley without any water or sense of direction in a car that's prone to overheating.

With a landscape like this, it's no wonder it's named Death Valley.
Photo: National Park Service.

Scott entertained many celebrities at the castle, including Will Rogers and William Randolph Hearst. When Johnson died, he gave the castle to a foundation, but Scotty was allowed to live in it, and he died there in 1954. Eventually the castle was sold to the National Park Service, which now gives daily tours of the house. Tour guides dress in period costumes to add a degree of authenticity for visitors, while revealing the story of duplicity behind the home's misleading name.

For more information call (760) 786–2395.

MILITARY SECRETS IN PLANE VIEW
Edwards Air Force Base

The motto of the Edwards Air Force Base is "Higher, Farther, Faster," and it is certainly well-earned. More historical flights have been launched at this 470-square-mile base in the western Mojave Desert than at any other place on earth.

Here Chuck Yeager hurtled into history by shattering the myth of the sound barrier on October 14, 1947, breaking that milestone in a rocket-powered Bell X-1. A lesser-known "first in flight" occurred here in 1977, when a Boeing 747 took off with the space shuttle *Enterprise* strapped to its back, soaring into the sky as the heaviest single unit to fly in aviation history.

The base's site was chosen for two good reasons: Its out-of-the-way location makes it easier from a security standpoint, and the surrounding dry lake beds provide an excellent and forgiving landing strip for the hundreds of experimental craft that have touched down here. Rogers Dry Lake, on the base, was named a National Historic Landmark in 1985.

Some of the Cold War–era craft that were formerly closely guarded military secrets are now displayed at the base's Flight Test Center Museum. Included is Yeager's sonic-buster, which hangs from a museum rafter. Other displays tell the history of Edwards and its record-breaking flights. The museum, located at 405 South Rosamond Boulevard, is currently closed to the public for security reasons but remains open to people who have official business at the base.

At a base annex museum in nearby Palmdale, the Blackbird Airpark offers a close-up view of two of the world's fastest and highest-flying planes, the A-12 and the SR-71A.

For more information on scheduling tours, call (661) 277–8050.

A Truly Underground Artist
Fresno

Baldasare Forestiere came to the United States from Sicily and worked as a "sandhog," digging underground to help build a Boston subway and New York's Holland Tunnel. He dreamed of a future aboveground, though, trekking to California and buying several acres of land he hoped to farm. Fate, however, sent him back underground.

The California land he bought turned out to be what's known around Fresno as hardpan, stony earth hardly suitable for farming. Undeterred, Forestiere started digging a hole for himself about 20 feet underground and discovered that at this depth the soil, and living, were to his satisfaction. He tunneled for almost the next forty years until his death in 1946 at age sixty-seven. In that time he created a subterranean wonderland that includes living quarters, gardens, skylights, courtyards, a chapel, and even a glass-bottomed fish pond. He also planted many fruit trees, carving holes in the soil overhead so that they could be nurtured with rain and light.

A lifelong bachelor, Forestiere reportedly once courted a

EXPOSING THE HISTORY OF BURLESQUE

When Dixie Evans performed as a burlesque dancer decades ago, the term "striptease artist" was an appropriate one. There was artistry in the way dancers used choreography, elaborate costumes, and humor in their acts. And there was more accent on the tease than the actual stripping in the grand era of burlesque, which ran from the 1930s to the 1950s. Dancers tantalized audiences by seductively strutting behind an array of props including fans, pasties, and G-strings.

That all gave way in the 1960s to what Evans and others feel is a more crass and full-frontal form of the sexy entertainment, sending many burlesque queens into retirement and signaling the end to this exotic chapter in American history.

That golden age of burlesque is laid bare in a unique exhibit hall on a former goat farm in Helendale in the Mojave Desert run by Evans, the boa-draped hostess of the Exotic World Burlesque Museum. Evans took over the collection in 1989, when her friend, former burlesque star Jennie Lee, died. (Lee was known in her day as the Bazoom Girl because she could endlessly twirl tassels with her bosom and behind.)

The collection includes artifacts from many of the stars of American burlesque, including Gypsy Rose Lee's glove collection, ivory-handled fans from Sally Rand, and assorted costumes and props from the likes of Blaze Starr, Lili St. Cyr, and Chesty Morgan. The museum is also a wonderful source of trivia where you can learn that the G-string got its name because it's the thinnest string on the violin and that Tempest Storm was the only burlesque star to ever perform at Carnegie Hall.

Tempest Storm is one of the many performers celebrated at Exotic World. Photo: Courtesy of Exotic World.

The museum hosts the annual *Miss Exotic World* contest, which features dancers ages twenty through their eighties who re-create the feel of burlesque dancing and vie for the crown of *Miss Exotic World*. For visitors who want to gawk at history, the contest is held the first Saturday every June. For more information call (760) 243–5261 or visit *Exotic World's* Web site at *www.exoticworldusa.org.*

young woman, but she wouldn't agree to live underground with him. Her rejection spurred him to dig on with a vengeance, or so the story goes.

After he died, a promoter lured tourists to the site by characterizing him as the freakish Mole Man. Now family members have restored the site, called Forestiere's Underground Gardens, and give weekend tours and even lease the place for weddings and business meetings.

For more information call (559) 271–0734.

DOUBLE DOSE OF BIG
Kingsburg

Kingsburg boasts not one but two gigantic attractions. That's noteworthy for the small town of 10,000 settled in 1886 by Swedish immigrants who had fled the Midwest seeking a warmer place to live.

As a tribute to the town's Swedish roots, Kingsburg's 1911 vintage water tower was transformed in 1985 into one of the world's largest coffeepots. It's 122 feet tall, visible for miles, and could hold up to 60,000 gallons of coffee, except that it's still used as a water tower. The colorful design is reminiscent of Swedish-peasant painting styles, and the pot itself pays tribute to the fact that Swedes do love their coffee.

In the early 1900s the town was more than 95 percent Swedish. Scandinavian influences are still felt in town, which hosts an annual Swedish festival the third weekend in May.

The town is also home to Sun-Maid Corporation headquarters, which features the world's largest box of raisins, recognized by the *Guinness Book of World Records* in 1992. California State University at Fresno students made the 12-foot-

high box and filled it with 16,500 pounds of raisins, in recognition of one of the region's major crops. The box is now empty,
but the town is full of pride over its two colossal relics.

A Granite Face That Directors Just Love

Lone Pine

First-time visitors to the Alabama Hills often feel a strong
sense of déjà vu, and rightly so. That's because chances are
they've seen this place before, as it has been the featured background to more than 300 feature films. The area's craggy
granite outcroppings and rugged terrain first attracted Hollywood in 1920, when Paramount made the silent film *The
Round Up,* starring Fatty Arbuckle. Film crews built roads and
trudged equipment up here many more times to capture scenes
from other westerns and dramatic films, earning the area the
nickname "Movie Flats."

Roy Rogers, Gene Autry, and Hopalong Cassidy worked on
pictures here, and later so did Cary Grant, Gregory Peck, and
Clint Eastwood. The cops chased Humphrey Bogart through
the Alabama Hills in *High Sierra.* More recently action scenes
from *Gladiator* were shot here, giving the unusual landscape
yet more screen time.

There aren't many communities that can throw a film festival
featuring nothing but movies shot right in its own backyard, but
Lone Pine can. Since 1990, the community has held the Lone
Pine Film Festival every Columbus Day weekend. The event features panel discussions, concerts, crafts shows, wagon rides,
and, of course, screenings of many of the films featuring the
Alabama Hills as a backdrop. There are also bus tours of famous
movie locations. For more information call (760) 876–9103.

THE BRIEF CHARGE OF THE CAMEL CORPS

Think of large animals of the Wild West, and images of horses and buffalo come to mind. Certainly not camels, but the beasts of burden with the foul breath and legendary hydration had their moment in American history.

In the 1850s the U.S. Congress, at the direction of then Secretary of War Jefferson Davis, authorized $30,000 to fund a U.S. Camel Corps. About twenty-five Mediterranean camels were brought to the United States to provide more efficient transport of supplies to remote western military posts.

Led by Edward Beale and assisted by camel experts "Greek George" Caralambo and Hadji "Hi Jolly" Ali, the strange caravan of soldiers and camels set out in 1857 from New Mexico heading to Los Angeles, with the goal of surveying a road along the way that would eventually become the famed Route 66.

The camels eventually arrived in Fort Tejon, a military garrison 70 miles north of Los Angeles near Lebec. The journey met with mixed results: The camels tended to spook the other pack animals and make their riders seasick, but they didn't stampede and could carry hundreds of pounds of supplies.

Beale had high hopes for the future of The Camel Corps, but the start of the Civil War diminished interest in the camels. They stayed at the fort for a few months and then were driven back to Los Angeles and sold. Some were set loose in the desert. Soon after, scary stories were being told in mining camps of a mysterious beast with red fur that became known as the Red Ghost. Eventually the strange beast was revealed to be a wayward camel from the disbanded corps.

Fort Tejon is now a state historic park with restored barracks, a tangible link to the country's long-forgotten experiment with military camels.

DUNES WITH TUNES
Mojave National Preserve

No one would think twice if you said you were heading out to the desert to hear a concert. After all, most people would assume you meant Las Vegas, with its many high-profile venues and headliner performers. But some tonal purists head to the Mojave for a musical performance of a much different sort, minus the Vegas glitter and big-name stars. The musical artist here is the Kelso Dunes, otherwise known as the Singing Sands.

Even if the dunes weren't musically inclined, they would be impressive enough. The Dunes rise more than 600 feet above the desert floor and emanate an ethereal golden glow. Until recently scientists couldn't figure how the dunes got there, because no new sand was found to be drifting into the area. Scientists finally

Listen up, because these dunes can sing. Photo: National Park Service.

determined that sand particles blown in from the nearby
Mojave River sink gave rise to the dunes over a period of some
25,000 years.

Not so easily explained are the impromptu concerts put on
by the dunes. Most often people report hearing booming noises;
some say they also hear musical instruments, bells, or drums;
others note the sound of trumpets. For centuries desert travelers around the world have reported hearing similar eerie
sounds. The most likely source is vibrations caused by shifting
sand particles, but less-scientific types just sit back and enjoy
the spiritual serenity of sand that sings.

A TOWN THAT REALLY ROCKS
Parkfield

Most towns wouldn't appreciate having their biggest fault
subjected to worldwide scrutiny. In the case of Parkfield,
though, that's exactly what has happened.

The town sits right on the San Andreas Fault, one of the
world's most notorious earthquake generators. And because
large quakes hit so regularly here, scientists are fixated with
the town's fault-line activity.

The U.S. Geological Survey initiated what's known as the
Parkfield Experiment in 1985, setting up sophisticated seismic
monitoring devices around town in the hope of catching a
major quake in the act. They're still waiting, but they've been
collecting scores of data that's being shared with earthquake
experts from all over. The idea here is that by "trapping" an
earthquake while it happens, scientists will learn more about
the nature of predicting them.

Parkfield is a prime spot to hang out waiting for the earth
to move. Since 1857, there have been six quakes of magnitude

6.0 or greater, the last occurring in 1966, and scores of lesser-sized shakers.

The town's eighteen residents, who have declared Parkfield the earthquake capital of the world, await the next big one with equal measures of pride and humor. No one is much worried about the consequences if one hits; after all, there aren't many buildings to knock over. Downtown consists mostly of an inn and a coffee shop, where diners can browse menus that playfully refer to desserts as "aftershocks." And as for all the geeky scientists coming into town to check on their equipment and study the town's fault, well, that's just good for local business.

COOL CAVERNS
Providence Mountains

Jack Mitchell headed a profitable real-estate company in Los Angeles in the 1920s. When the Depression hit in the 1930s and ruined business, he became interested in a land venture of an entirely different sort.

Mitchell learned about sensational limestone caverns in the Providence Mountains of the Mojave Desert, so he staked out mining claims in the area to gain control of the land. He opened the caves in 1932, hoping to run a successful business by offering public tours.

The unique caverns feature dramatic formations of stalagmites and stalactites and offer something else of interest to desert tourists—they remain a constant, comfortable 65 degrees, no matter what the temperature is outside.

The three caverns that Mitchell named are the El Pakiva, or devil's house, Tecopa, after a Shoshonean chief, and the Winding Stair Cave. In Mitchell's day, visitors had to scramble around the caves, sometimes in the dark, until tour leaders would toss in flares to light the way. The caverns, which are the only limestone caverns in California, were eventually bought by the state in 1954 and now have lighting and stairs.

Mitchell Caverns, as they are now called, received unexpected publicity in 1991 when they were used in filming of Oliver Stone's *The Doors*. Stone received permission to paint on the cave walls more than one hundred pictographs designed to look like prehistoric drawings. They were designed as background for a scene in which Jim Morrison visits a holy man in a cave. The drawings were supposed to have been done with a powder that could be easily vacuumed off after the shoot, but somehow water got into the mix, and the images seeped into the cave walls. Oops.

Publicity about the gaffe, and release of the movie, generated a surge in public interest in the caves. The pictographs were eventually removed with minimal damage. You can make reservations for a tour by calling (760) 928–2586.

IT'S A JUNGLE IN THERE
Rosamond

The big cats at the Exotic Feline Breeding Compound look playful enough. They roll over and rub up against a tree trunk and appear as good-natured and cuddly as any household pet. But don't be fooled. They're the real deal, as potentially deadly and powerful as any ferocious jaguar or cougar in the wild.

They're here in this desert facility near an abandoned gold mine and a huge air base for their own protection, not ours. The sixty or so big cats are all endangered in the wild.

Joseph Maynard opened the center in 1977 as a breeding facility. The center now houses sixteen species of cat, including leopards, jaguars, tigers, ocelots, and bobcats. Zoos around the world respect the center's reputation as a breeding facility and often send their cats here to mate. The desert solitude and rural surroundings, apparently, are conducive to feline frolicking. The birth of an exotic cub is a routine event here.

The facility began inviting visitors in 1983, and it's nothing like your average zoo experience. Guests can sometimes walk within 5 feet of these exotic creatures, separated only by a fence. Some of the more high-strung cats are kept away from the public for obvious reasons. If you'd like the true jungle experience, the center is open occasionally during twilight hours, when the cats are most active. Drop by, if you dare.

Call ahead with questions at (661) 256–3793.

Waiting a Long Time for Their Closeup
Searles Valley

Some people become movie stars overnight, but it took much longer for the Trona Pinnacles to reach the big screen. The Pinnacles were shaped by 100,000 years of evolution before they caught the eye of Hollywood producers.

The Pinnacles are 500 oddly shaped spires set in a desert wilderness against majestic mountains, a landscape that is decidedly otherworldly. It's no wonder that the Pinnacles have served as an alien backdrop for a number of science-fiction films, including *Star Trek V: The Final Frontier,* the remake of *Planet of the Apes,* and the television series *Lost in Space.* Why build an eerie landscape when nature has already created one for you? The Pinnacles have been featured in about a dozen movies and television series as well as countless commercial shoots.

It took thousands of years to create a landscape this weird. Photo: Alcarine Power.

The Trona Pinnacles, in the Western Mojave Desert, are the country's best example of tufa formations, consisting of calcium carbonate. The Pinnacles were formed when the area was underwater as part of a long chain of mineral-rich lakes that stretched from Mono Lake to Death Valley. They are more like coral reefs than rock and can be very brittle. To help ensure their protection, they were declared a National Natural Landscape and are under the supervision of the U.S. Bureau of Land Management.

Honoring the Grapes of Wrinkle
Selma

For most of us it's hard to work up much enthusiasm for a piece of shriveled fruit. Not so for the folks of Selma. Since 1963, this agricultural city has proudly associated itself with the dried-up grape we commonly call a raisin. Selma is the self-proclaimed raisin capital of the world.

Selma originally was the Home of the Peach, but the peach crop soured, and the raisin was embraced, and for good reason. The area produces about 90 percent of the world's supply of the minuscule sweet treat, and for Selma that's cause for celebration. The city hosts the annual Raisin Festival, which features the crowning of the Raisin Queen, carnival rides, and, of course, lots or raisin-theme foods, such as raisin-pecan pie and raisin-sweet-potato turnovers.

Selma grabbed the title of raisin capital first, but residents of nearby communities sometimes grumble that any town in the Fresno region could make the same claim. But Selma has fiercely defended its title. In the 1980s, when a CBS miniseries called *Fresno* aired and labeled Fresno the raisin capital of the world, citizens of Selma howled in protest, pointing out that they were king of the raisin heap. Show producers withered under the heat of the complaints and smoothed things over by referring to Fresno as the "raisin basket of the world."

Just try wrapping your arms around the General Sherman Tree.
Photo: National Park Service.

CAN'T SEE THE FOREST PAST THIS TREE

*H*ow big is the General Sherman Tree in Sequoia National Park? Its biggest branch is bigger than most any other trees. You could park an SUV on some of its larger branches, if you could get it up there. The General stands almost 275 feet tall and is noted for being the largest tree by volume in the world. Some claim that it's the largest living thing in the world, but picky scientists dispute that, pointing to other organisms such as a large fungus in Washington state that's even larger. If the General and the fungus went head-to-head in battle though, say in some reality-TV program, the General could dispatch the fungus with a gentle swat of one of its minor branches.

The General Sherman Tree didn't just happen overnight with a sudden growth spurt; it is more than 2,100 years in the making. Its circumference is a jaw-dropping 103 feet, and its estimated weight is 2.7 million pounds.

The colossal tree is a major reason why more than one million visitors head to the park annually. Another celebrity trunk in the park is the immense General Grant Tree, designated as the National Christmas Tree in 1926. It's hardly dwarfed by the General Sherman Tree as it's only about 8 feet lower in height. Both trees are known in scientific circles as Sequoiadendron giganteum. *In lay terms that means one heck of a big tree.*

A TRACK THAT THROWS TRAINS FOR A LOOP
Tehachapi

If there's a Holy Grail of Rail for train enthusiasts, it's the famed Tehachapi Loop. The nineteenth-century engineering marvel solved a major challenge: how to get massive trains chugging over the 4,000-foot summit without having them climb too steep a grade. The answer was a tunnel that takes trains through a tight counterclockwise loop so that the front of the train emerges in the unusual position of passing over its rear section. For a few moments, in fact, the train's locomotive heads in the opposite direction of its caboose, although the whole train remains on the same track.

This unusual design is enough to draw train lovers from around the world, who snap photos of the odd rail course or just sit back and watch the trains in action. About sixty or so trains pass by each day, making Tehachapi the nation's busiest single-track line. It connects rail lines between Northern and Southern California.

In all, the mountain track, completed in 1876, has eighteen tunnels and is more than 8,000 feet long. The track is celebrated in many ways in town, including a 60-foot-wide mural that depicts the loop and frequent model-train displays presented by the Tehachapi Loop Railroad Club. Plans call for a rail museum at the refurbished train station. There is a viewing area of the loop about 8 miles west of town on Tehachapi-Woodford Road. Or you can see it on a Web cam at www.train orders.com/cameras/tehachapi/.

THE LAST WORD ON MIRACLE CURES

*T*o high rollers motoring across the desert terrain of Interstate 15 on their way to Las Vegas, passing the exit sign for the town of Zzyzx is merely a curious roadside distraction. Travelers whiz by, focused on getting well at the casino tables miles ahead in Nevada. Not long ago, however, tourists flocked to Zzyzx for their salvation, seeking miracle cures for everything from baldness to cancer.

Self-styled radio evangelist Curtis Springer created the Zzyzx Mineral Springs and Health Resort in 1944, hiring cheap labor from Los Angeles' Skid Row to erect a town devoted to Springer's unique vision of spirituality and a vigorous lifestyle. The grounds featured a sixty-room hotel called the Castle, a cross-shaped swimming pool, a man-made lake, and indoor baths along a main street named the Boulevard of Dreams. Springer called it Zzyzx for the obvious reason: He wanted his resort to be listed last in the phone book.

For three decades thousands of visitors came to listen to Springer's sermons and take cures in mineral and mud baths. They dined on his purported curative cuisine at the resort's main dining hall and took home a multitude of elixirs, including something called a Hollywood Pep Cocktail. Springer's sermons and promotions for his resort and products were aired on hundreds of radio stations in the United States and abroad, producing a steady stream of customers.

Criticism by the American Medical Association and federal charges of false advertising and unauthorized use of federal land led to Springer's eviction and the closing of the resort in 1974. The grounds are now devoted to a much more scientifically based endeavor as the home of the California Desert Studies Center, a Cal State University field station that features science labs and offers classes to the public.

A DIG AT CONVENTIONAL WISDOM
Yermo

Prevailing scientific theory is that the first humans arrived in the Americas sometime between 10,000 and 12,000 years ago, crossing over a land bridge from Asia. Supporters of a little-known archaeological site in this Mojave Desert town have a major bone of contention with this notion. That's because evidence unearthed here indicates that humans may have been here much earlier than that—more than 200,000 years ago, in fact, if their archaeological detective work is right.

The site first drew attention in 1942, when an amateur archaeologist came across what looked like stone tools. This find got the attention of Ruth Simpson, a curator at the Southwest Museum of Los Angeles, who eventually brought in Dr. Louis Leakey. Leakey was no slouch when it came to dating archaeological sites, having already earned fame for excavation work at an Early Man site in Tanzania. Leakey began digging near Yermo in 1963 and continued as project supervisor until his death in 1972. Thousands of primitive stone tools, including hammers and scrapers, have been discovered, and scientific dating says they're about 200,000 years old, making the site the most significant find in North America.

Problem is, the archaeological establishment hasn't recognized the site's authenticity. Some scoff at the idea that humans were there that long ago and say the rock shapes are the result of natural causes, not human crafting of tools. And they point out that no human remains have been found here.

Since Leakey's death, others have continued the work at what's now called the Calico Early Man Site. A small visitor center here displays some of the artifacts, and guided tours are offered at various times from Wednesday through Sunday. To uncover more information call the Bureau of Land Management Field office at (760) 252–6000 or visit on the Web at www.ca.blm.gov/barstow/calico.html.

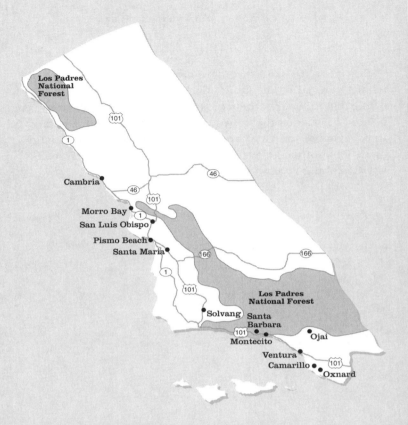

Los Padres
National
Forest

101

1

Cambria

46

46

101

Morro Bay
San Luis Obispo
1

Pismo Beach
Santa Maria

166

166

1

101

Solvang
Santa
Barbara

Los Padres
National Forest

Montecito
101

Ojai

Ventura
Camarillo
101

Oxnard

CENTRAL COAST

Central Coast

THIS COLLECTION IS FOR THE BIRDS
Camarillo

In 1992 Rene Corado set out to transport some eggs from Los Angeles to Camarillo. The trip took him seven months. You see, he had to make several trips because the shipment involved a total of more than one million eggs. To put that in perspective, if you took all those eggs and laid them end to end, they would cover a distance of, well, let's just say it would be farther than a chicken could walk in a day.

The eggs were destined for the new home of the Western Foundation of Vertebrate Zoology, which boasts one of the world's largest collections of eggs. All told, it houses more than 190,000 sets of eggs from about 4,000 bird species. The foundation also has more than 18,000 nests, the largest such collection in the world, and 53,000 bird skins. This extraordinary ornithological collection is displayed in drawers contained in large white specimen cabinets in a warehouse space in an industrial area. Each egg, nest, and bird skin is documented with detailed information about where and how it was found, including the weather at the time. "Ultimately, the collection tells scientists how these birds lived," says foundation director Linnea Hall.

The foundation founder is Ed Harrison, a Los Angeles real-estate and oil magnate who was an avid wildlife collector with a fondness for birds. He amassed more than 11,000 egg sets and 2,000 nests, which he stored in his Los Angeles home and office before the collection was moved, very carefully, to Camarillo.

The nonprofit foundation is an invaluable resource for researchers interested in bird conservation. Access to the collection is mostly open to, well, egghead science types as well as educators. The general public can schedule tours by appointment only by calling (805) 388–9944. Surf over to www.wfvz.org for more information.

THE CENTRAL COAST'S OTHER CASTLE
Cambria

Thousands of visitors come each year to San Simeon to marvel at Hearst Castle, the spectacular mansion built for William Randolph Hearst. But just a few miles away in tony Cambria is a castle of a different sort. Art Beal's Nit Wit Ridge is in a realm decidedly different from Hearst's extravagantly outfitted property. Hearst scoured the world for the finest materials and furnishings for his abode, whereas Beal constructed his startling residence mostly from junk.

Beginning in 1928 and for the next fifty years, Beal used hand tools and his zany imagination to adorn his three-story dwelling with items such as worn car tires and rims, antique stoves, driftwood, abalone shells, discarded TV antennas, and old toys. He decorated one arch with military shells. Used toilet seats served as picture frames on the wall. Beal designated a spiral staircase as his "California refrigerator," storing items there that needed cooling because it remained at 50 degrees, thanks to a nice breeze.

"He didn't want to conform. He was kind of rebellious," says Michael O'Malley, who bought the property in 1999 with his wife, Stacey. "He wasn't eccentric or mysterious. He was kind of a comedian."

Art Beal's house of trash draws plenty of curious visitors.
Photo: Stacey O'Malley.

Beal worked as a plumber and an abalone diver at times and in later life was heralded as an extraordinary folk artist. Officials recognized the house as a State Historic Landmark, commending him for using a "blend of native materials and contemporary elements" and for his "unique cosmic humor and zest for life."

Some disenchanted locals refer to Beal's creation as the trash house and wish that it would just go away. But the O'Malleys are committed to preserving the landmark and now offer free tours. They've cleaned up the property but haven't touched much inside. Visitors can see Beal's canned goods on shelves and view his clothes hanging in the closet. If you'd like to see what results when one man brings the garbage *into* the house, call (805) 927–2690 to schedule a visit.

DIVA WITH A GREEN THUMB
Montecito

She was born Hanna Puacz in Poland but became an opera singer who took the stage name Madame Ganna Walska. She toured Europe and America in the early twentieth century and became more known as a socialite who married well—six times, in fact. Madame Walska settled in California, and on the advice of her last husband, she purchased a thirty-seven-acre estate in Montecito in 1941 that had formerly been a commercial nursery. Then she divorced for the final time and spent the next four decades creating a fantastic landscape of exotic trees and plants, befitting her operatic flair for the dramatic.

At first Walska called her estate Tibetland, intending it as a retreat for Tibetan monks. But the monks never retreated to her residence, so she named it Lotusland, in honor of the sacred Indian lotus plant growing in a pond.

Walska's tastes in the garden were worthy of a diva. She cultivated only the best and the biggest, the rare and the unusual. She planted many odd-looking plants and trees to create a fairyland of shapes and colors.

Lotusland contains more than a dozen separate garden areas, each built around a theme. The Blue Garden features Blue Atlas Cedars, soaring Chilean wine palms, and other plants with silver and blue-gray leaves. An aloe garden contains more than 120 different kinds of aloe plants and a pool with a giant clamshell fountain. Lotusland's collection of cycads, rare and prehistoric ancestors to the palm, is considered one of the biggest such displays in the United States. There are more than 175 different kinds of cycads represented here, some extinct in the wild and most endangered.

Tours are available by reservation only and fill up well in advance. To book your visit call (805) 969–9990 or take a virtual stroll at www.lotusland.org.

Ganna Walska had an opera career before turning to exotic gardening.
Photo: Lotusland Archives.

BRAWNY PAWNS
Morro Bay

Chess players need an agile mind and a beefy physique to succeed in this town. The best strategies collapse if players can't hoist a key piece into position, and that's a real challenge here, because some of them weigh thirty pounds. Morro Bay's Giant Chessboard turns the brainy game into a recreational sport. With waist-high wooden pieces measuring a foot in diameter, the game challenges players to not only know where a piece should go but to have the muscles to get it there.

Longtime resident and music teacher Botso Korisheli convinced the city to sponsor the giant board in the 1970s after he saw similar ones in many open-air chess parks while he was living in Europe. He designed it, the city donated the redwood lumber, and a friend carved the set with a special lathe. A cement board, which Korisheli guesses is about 30 feet by 30 feet, was dedicated in 1976 in a small downtown park, and the giant board has been a local oddity and resource ever since. It's the site of many chess tournaments and a hangout for the local chess club. The public can play by reserving the pieces through the Recreation Department.

"Sometimes people complain that the pieces are too heavy. But it's a good exercise. I call it brain gymnastics," Korisheli says. Local chess player Bruce Risley has been playing there since it opened. "It's dazzling, and it's also puzzling," he says. "The perspective is so different that you have to get used to it." A few years back, Risley says he didn't mind the weight of the pieces. "Now I notice it more," he says.

To plan your giant game of chess, call (805) 772–6278.

A SOFT SHELL
Morro Bay

Dave Thomas sells seashells by the seashore, and he has been doing it since 1952. Some kids sell lemonade. Dave sold shells, setting up a stand on family land in downtown Morro Bay and offering abalone shells given to him by his father, a commercial fisherman, for 10 cents a piece. He made $100 that first summer.

Dave Thomas has a shell or two for you.

Photo: Justine Thomas.

"That was worth a lot more then," he says with a laugh. With the help of his parents, his stand grew into a real shop in 1962, leading Thomas to a life of the soft and hard shell.

A trip to Thomas's aptly named Shell Shop is like a science-class field trip. The store features hundreds of varieties of marine seashells from more than thirty different countries. The biggest shells are 600-pound giant clamshells from the South Pacific; the smallest are ⅛ inch. There are shell-themed jewelry and crafts too, including wood chimes, chandeliers, and decorative boxes.

Thomas has traveled to faraway places in the pursuit of shells, and he's grateful for the experience. He says that each trip is always a surprise, from the people he meets to the stock that's available. Shells have seasons, and sometimes he won't know what's available until he gets to a destination. "It's not like buying a case of soup," he says of the shell business.

Though times have changed since Thomas sold his first abalone shell, one tradition still stands: He offers some shells for 5 cents, a favorite with youngsters. "It's getting hard to do that because the bag costs more than a penny," he explains. If you want to sift through hundreds of colorful shells, drop by The Shell Shop at 590 Embarcadero or call (805) 772–8014.

THE BOOK ON HONESTY
Ojai

Bart's Books has everything a book lover could want: a great selection of new and used books, knowledgeable helpers, good prices, and lots of browsing space—everything, it seems, but a roof.

Inspired by the open bookstalls on the Parisian Left Bank when it was opened in 1964, Bart's Books is probably the

How about a book on building a roof?

largest open-air bookstore in America. Books are stacked in cubbyholes, drawers, and shelves, spaced around two court-yards squeezed between a house and garage. For added atmosphere a venerable oak tree grows right inside the retail space.

Though most customers marvel at the store's layout, they also ponder the obvious question: What happens when it rains? That's all figured out. Outdoor shelves here face south and west, which protect them from most storms, which come from the north. Tarps cover up any exposed books. More expensive works, like first editions, are kept indoors in galleries in the garage and house.

The store also has an unusual honesty policy. Dozens of used books are stacked in wooden shelves outside the store even after it closes for the day. Customers who drop by after hours and find something they like are asked to push the required money through a front-door slot. This tradition started with the store's first owner and continues to this day, although the store has changed hands a few times. Some shop owners would laugh at the idea of running a business on the honor system, but locals point with pride at Bart's trusting policy as representative of the town's laid-back and humane spirit.

Current owner Gary Schlichter has stacked the store with a healthy supply of occult and metaphysical books and hosts an annual psychic fair at the store. Perhaps he believes he can use ESP to track down any customers who subvert the store's honor system.

Bart's Books is at 302 West Matilija Street; the phone number is (805) 646–3755.

THIS MAN FIGURES TO TELL SOME STORIES
Ojai

George Stuart has devoted more than five decades to putting a face on history—actually dozens of faces and the bodies to go with them. Stuart has meticulously crafted more than 400 miniature figures of prominent people in world history, from early Romans to America's Founding Fathers.

These figures aren't simple models but complex reconstructions down to receding chins and elaborate hairdos as well as authentic accessories such as swords and jewelry. He makes a detailed study before making each work out of metal, wood, clay, leather, and other materials. "I use everything I can get my hands on, including death masks, autopsy reports, portraits, and biographical descriptions," he says.

Theses figures bring history to life for storyteller and artist George Stuart.
Photo: Peter D'Aprix.

Stuart is an entertainer who long ago forged a career as a storyteller. He developed his first figure in 1953 to help illustrate a lecture, and he has been creating them ever since. Familiar names in his collection include Marie Antoinette, Abraham Lincoln, and Thomas Jefferson. There are members of the Ming Dynasty of China as well as the French royal family. He says working on a scale of 3 inches to the foot seems to be the most appropriate size.

His figures and lectures undoubtedly help teach people history, a field of study most Americans are decidedly "unlearned in," he observes. But his real motivation, he admits, is to make money. He has patented his works as George Stuart's Historical Figures. He works on commission and displays works at his Ojai gallery, which is open to the public on Saturday and Sunday. Or you can stop by the Ventura County Museum of History and Art, which exhibits many of Stuart's historical figures. For more information visit Stuart's Web site at www.galleryhistoricalfigures.com or call (805) 646–6574.

IN THE PINK
Ojai

Ojai is a mecca for free spirits bent on doing things their own way. It's no different when it comes to watching sunsets. Though most people look west, naturally, the folks here turn their gaze to the east.

They have their reasons, of course. They're looking for what's known in these parts as the Pink Moment, when the sun's rays bathe the Topa Topa Mountain in a dazzling pastel glow. The moment comes at dusk, and when they say "moment," they mean it. It's a fleeting phenomenon but one that's worth the wait. If there's one thing everyone knows around this town, it's the time each day of the Pink Moment. If they don't, it's published daily in the local paper.

Even without the momentary pinkness, the views here are stunning. So much so that when filmmakers needed a stand-in for the mythical paradise of Shangri-La while making the 1937 film *Lost Horizon,* they didn't try and create a set. They simply packed up their equipment and headed for the Ojai Valley to shoot their movie.

Residents and visitors here can experience paradise any time of day, Pink Moment or not.

GOING BANANAS OVER STRAWBERRIES
Oxnard

There's no reason why you would want to do this, but if you placed every strawberry grown annually in California side by side they would create a fruity necklace that would wrap around the globe fifteen times. Got the picture? Strawberries are berry, berry big in California, and especially Ventura County, which grows a quarter of the state's output. More than ten million baskets are shipped daily from the region during peak growing season from April to June, generating more than $231 million in annual revenues.

That's cause for celebration in Oxnard. Since 1984, the city has hosted the California Strawberry Festival, offering visitors a chance to see what happens when cooks get a little fruity inventing strawberry-themed dishes, including pizzas, nachos, kabobs, and even barbecue sandwiches topped with, um, straw-berry sauce. For the less adventurous there are baskets of the plain fruit available as well as traditional fare such as straw-berry shortcake.

This is probably not the best way to eat tarts at the California Strawberry Festival. Photo: Courtesy of California Strawberry Festival.

Watch out for flying strawberry pies aimed at volunteer victims perched in wooden cutouts, an event known as the tart toss. Persons who don't mind shoving their face into a mound of whipped cream can enter the strawberry-shortcake eating contest, a truly messy showdown.

The festival is held in May on seventy-five scenic acres of Strawberry Meadows of College Park at 3250 South Rose Avenue. Call (888) 288–9242 for exact dates or visit the festival Web site at www.strawberry-fest.org, where you can learn such berry trivia as the fact that there are about 200 seeds in every strawberry and that the origin of the berry's name may have come because it was originally sold in baskets made of grass straws.

A DISAPPEARING CLAM ACT
Pismo Beach

Locals fondly remember Pismo's glory days of clamming when the clams were bigger than your hand and so abundant that the population was estimated in the millions. One popular method of clamming then was to scoop them up by the hundreds by dragging the beach with a horse-driven plow. Not only were Pismo clams stoutly sized—around 7 inches in diameter—they were tasty, too. It's no wonder the city proudly proclaimed itself the clam capital of the world.

But by the 1990s the clam population had, well, clammed up. Nary a clam could be found, except for a few scrawny ones here or there, too small to legally catch.

Some blame overharvesting. Others point fingers at sea otters that gobbled up Pismo clams by the flipperful, smashing the shells together to get at the succulent meat inside.

A DIG AT FUTURE ARCHAEOLOGISTS

*A*n ancient Egyptian city is buried deep somewhere in the sweeping sand dunes of California's Central Coast, but there's a logical explanation for such an oddball archaeological site. For the city was never a real place but rather a famous movie set.

In 1923 Cecil B. DeMille filmed his silent biblical epic The Ten Commandments in true DeMille style—lavishly produced and overbudget. The film's whopping $1.4-million cost was outrageous for that era of moviemaking. The set was colossal, including twenty-one sphinxes that weighed five tons each and four Pharaoh statues that measured three stories tall. The city also included a 110-foot-high wall covered with hieroglyphics. More than 1,500 construction workers labored to create what is still regarded as one of the largest concrete-and-plaster sets ever built.

When filming ended, DeMille ordered the massive set buried in the sand where filming took place, somewhere within the coastal preserve now known as the Guadalupe-Nipomo Dunes. Historians suggest that DeMille hoped to tweak the minds of future archaeologists who might uncover the remains and be duly puzzled at its incongruity. The simple reason for burial of the set might be that DeMille lacked funds to properly dismantle it or that he didn't want other filmmakers using it.

A group of film buffs and historians has worked over the last few years to locate the buried set with radar, but they still need to raise thousands of dollars to properly excavate it. At the Dunes Center at 1055 Guadalupe Street in Guadalupe, visitors can watch a video about DeMille's lost

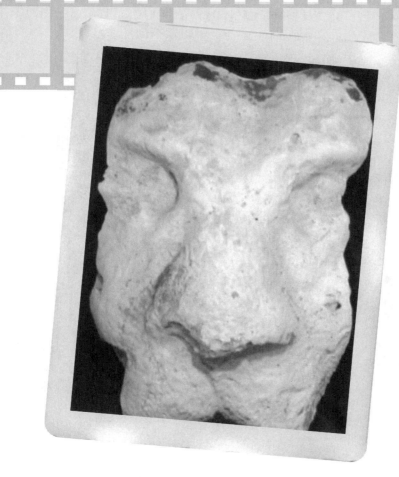

A lion's face from Pharaoh's throne, a recovered relic from DeMille's lost city.
Photo: Courtesy of Guadalupe-Nipomo Dunes Center.

city and can view relics that have been recovered, including part of the face of a lion statue and several cough-syrup bottles. According to the visitor-center's staff, workers used the cough-syrup bottles to smuggle alcohol onto the set during Prohibition, proof that they weren't shy about sinning while making a movie about the Ten Commandments.

The clam family comes out of its shell for the annual Clam Festival.
Photo: City of Pismo Beach.

Now clamming in Clam City is only for the truly adventurous. You need a salt-water fishing license and can only legally harvest clams that measure at least 4½ inches in diameter. It takes a lot of hard work and luck to get the legal limit of ten per day.

Clams are still celebrated here anyway at the annual Clam Festival, which includes a parade, the crowning of a clam queen, and a hotly-contested clam-chowder cookoff. The clams are imported from other areas, but the fun is all homespun. For more information on the clam festival, held each October, call the city's visitor information center at (800) 443–7778 or visit its Web site at www.classiccalifornia.com.

HEY DUDE, IT'S MIGRATION TIME
Pismo Beach

Monarch butterflies are magnificent flyers, sometimes covering up to 100 miles per day. They're also pretty savvy about picking their winter-vacation spot. At the first sign of cold weather, they flutter by the thousands to California beaches, some trekking from as far away as Canada. Descending upon their beach locale of choice, the butterflies pursue traditional activities of relaxing, snacking on nectar, warming themselves in the sun, and, of course, mating.

High on the monarch's list of favorite beach hangouts are the butterfly trees of Pismo Beach, a grove of eucalyptus and Monterey pines. The monarchs start arriving in late October and cluster in the trees with each insect hanging with its wings over the butterfly below, creating a cascading, dazzling pattern of yellow,

Monarch butterflies enjoy wintering
at California beaches.
Photo: City of Pismo Beach.

black, and orange. This is one of the largest monarch-migration sites in the country, with as many as 100,000 butterflies quivering in the trees throughout the winter months. After mating, females deposit eggs in milkweed plants, and caterpillars hatch out and then begin the metamorphosis into butterflies. By early spring they'll begin the long journey home, returning again when nature calls them back next fall.

The Monarch Butterfly Grove is located a half mile south of Pismo Beach off Highway 1. Guided tours are available during the season. For more information call the Pismo Beach Chamber of Commerce at (805) 773–4382.

THE GOOD VIBRATIONS OF VINYL
San Luis Obispo

Gary Freiberg was blown away when he first heard Bob Dylan's *Bringing It All Back Home* album. "That put a little turn in my road. Suddenly life got heavy," Freiberg recalls. He began writing poetry and expanding his horizons.

Music has always had a dynamic effect on Freiberg, and when he thinks music he thinks vinyl, as in the sometimes scratchy but warm sound from records spun on turntables. And he believes others do, too. "We have a unique relationship with vinyl, much more so than with tapes or CDs," he says. "Records represent chapters in people's lives."

Though technology has turned the phonograph needle into a relic, there are vinyl purists who have hung onto their albums, if only for the cover art and the memories they conjure up. So Freiberg came up with Vinyl Record Day, a celebration of bygone days of rpms and record skips. The event operates as if digital technology didn't exist. You won't find a CD anywhere—

Gary Freiberg has old music covered.
Photo: Mary Taylor.

just vendors hawking vintage albums and DJs spinning a variety of music on turntables, from Big Band to rock.

During the event Freiberg mounts a display of classic album
covers, which he says are becoming valuable collector items, even
if they don't contain the records once sold with them. Freiberg
and his wife have launched a company that sells a patented frame
designed to easily mount an album cover as art, available at
www.rockartpictureshow.com. For more information on Vinyl
Record Day, take a spin over to www.vinylrecordday.org.

LODGING A PLACE IN HISTORY

*T*he motel seems so practical and obvious you'd think it came into being on its own. But not so. Architect Arthur Heineman invented the concept of roadside quarters where weary travelers could drive right up to their rooms. In 1925 Heineman spent $80,000 to build a Spanish-style lodging with forty bungalows surrounding a courtyard in San Luis Obispo. He offered rooms for $2.00 a night, opening what historians agree is the world's first motel. Heineman is also credited with coining the term "motel" by combining the words hotel and motor. But passing drivers didn't recognize Heineman's cleverness with words. When they saw the sign to his Motel Inn, they just assumed he had misspelled hotel. So Heineman erected a neon sign that alternately flashed the words hotel and motel to clear up any confusion.

Workers took advantage of the motel's location at the bottom of a steep hill to pass out publicity brochures to passing motorists as they began a slow ascent up the incline in their clanking Model Ts.

Heineman envisioned a string of motels from San Diego to Seattle, but the Depression curbed his plans, and only the original inn was built. The historic motel closed in the early 1990s, but new owners plan to restore it.

STUCK ON TRADITION
San Luis Obispo

Visitors to this town's unconventional attraction often emit moans such as "Gross!" and "Eeew!" That's about right, considering what they're gawking at: a downtown alley with facing walls covered with mounds of chewed gum. It's as disgusting as it sounds, and yet it has been treated as a cherished monument for more than a half century. Historians say that teens in the 1950s began splattering chewed gum on the walls as artistic expressions. Others admired the effort and added to it until the walls were literally gummed up. Bubble Gum Alley was established.

Civic leaders have mixed feelings about the wadded walls. As yucky as they are, they do draw people to town. But every so often an antigum movement swells in the city, and sometimes action is taken. In 1996 the city ordered a high-pressure hose turned loose on the gummy surface, hoping to clean it up. The plan was for the gum to just wash away, but instead the hose shot mounds of it into the air, raining chunks of chewed gum on cars and people. So the hose was turned off, and the gummy alley survived.

This is one monument that is constantly evolving. Visitors are encouraged to add their wad to the stuck-on piles, and most comply. Some even try writing messages or creating designs, such as the American flag or flowers. If you'd like to stick up your contribution, the alley is located in the 700 block of Higuera Street between Garden and Broad.

A REST ROOM WITH A VIEW
San Luis Obispo

You don't often pass a urinal and think "photo opportunity," but such is the case with the men's room at the Madonna Inn. Travelers flock here not just for the pleasure of relieving themselves but also for the joy of viewing what many consider to be the world's most famous rest room, which features an 8-foot-wide stone waterfall as its centerpiece.

Owner Alex Madonna, who opened the hotel in 1958, estimates that one million people visit the rest room annually. It's certainly the only men's room endorsed by a local chamber of commerce as a place to visit. Men who go there to actually do their business might find privacy in short supply. More often women outnumber men in the grottolike environment, giggling and snapping pictures.

The rest of the inn is pretty photogenic, too. The whole place is done up in cotton-candy pink, and its 109 rooms are designed in over-the-top kitschy themes. Most famous is the Caveman Room, where guests can relax in the splendor of solid rock floors, wall and ceilings, and even a rock shower. The Matterhorn Room offers a taste of the Swiss Alps, whereas the Traveler's Yacht makes you feel as though you're in a boat.

The inn's steakhouse features circular pink booths, and the women's rest room boasts leather doors, crystal chandeliers, velvet-lined walls, and cherub faucet handles.

If you're passing through and want an interesting place for a road stop, pull into 100 Madonna Road. For longer stays call (800) 543–9666 for room reservations.

A CLUB THAT ENJOYS TOSSING OTHER CLUBS AROUND
Santa Barbara

Every week for the past several years, Matthew Thornley gets together with friends and begins tossing stuff in the air—mostly handled clubs but sometimes pieces of driftwood or assorted fruits and vegetables.

At the Jugglers Convention everything is up in the air.
Photo: Robert Bernstein.

This activity passes for fun at regular gatherings of the Santa Barbara Jugglers Association, whose members enjoy the challenge of keeping things up in the air. Aside from its weekly meetings, the group hosts an annual jugglers convention that Thornley says is probably the longest-running juggling festival in the United States held at the same location. Presented each April at the University of California at Santa Barbara gym, the Isla Vista Jugglers Convention is an informal celebration of the sport of multitasking. Amateurs and pros alike spend the day flipping all kinds of objects in the air, from balls to torches. Wanna-be jugglers can stop by for the daylong free forum and pick up some tips. At night there is a benefit performance for the local Rape Crisis Center.

Thornley says that new members can usually be juggling with some skill after thirty minutes of instruction. "We can get them throwing things in the right general direction in that time. But juggling takes a lifetime to master," Thornley says.

For more information on the club and festival, log onto www.sbjuggle.org.

DOGS IN FETCHING ATTIRE
Santa Barbara

California has always been a place where folks feel free to explore their identity. What's true of humans goes for their pets. Though dogs here are usually dogs, occasionally they are not. For there are special events where dogs are given the chance to step out of their fur, so to speak, and become, say, another animal. Or species even.

Pooches of all sizes and temperaments make tracks to Santa Barbara each year to participate in a major canine identity crisis known as the Big Dog Parade. Hundreds of mutts show up

Anyone seen my matching shoes?
Photo: Courtesy of Big Dog Sportswear.

to create a parade downtown that draws thousands of spectators. The only catch for the canine marchers: They can't go as dogs. Some come dressed as other creatures, such as lions, butterflies, rabbits, and even lobsters. Others portray food—one year the best-dressed costume went to a dachshund outfitted as a hot dog in a bun. Accompanying this truly haute dog were people costumed as jars of ketchup and mustard as well as a bag of fries. Some dogs wear wigs; others don bikinis. As we said, there's more room here for freedom of expression.

Sometimes owners dress up as dogs and their dogs dress up like people. Other dogs come as characters from whatever movie is hottest at parade time. In 2003, for example, dogs got to live out their *Matrix* fantasies.

Despite its name, the Big Dog Parade is open to mutts of all sizes. The name refers to its sponsor, Big Dog Sportswear, based in Santa Barbara. The company's flagship store was wiped out in a storm a few years back and began the parade in 1994 as a way to celebrate its reopening. Check out www.bigdogs.com for information on the annual event.

A MUSEUM THAT REALLY SLEIGHS 'EM
Santa Barbara

Nowadays horse-and-buggy rides are reserved for a unique conveyance at weddings or touristy trots around scenic vacation spots. It's easy to forget that not so long ago the humble horse-drawn carriage was a common mode of transport and not just some quaint relic with wheels.

Step into the Carriage and Western Art Museum and you'll once again experience life in the slow lane, when horsepower really meant how fast your horses could gallop. The museum exhibits more than fifty antique buggies, including the prover-

Antique hearse carriage, one of many exhibits at the Carriage and Western Art Museum.

bial surrey with a fringe on top. A circus wagon from the 1870s features gold-leaf wheels. There's a black hearse and a more cheery school-bus wagon with charcoal foot warmers that kept little feet toasty on the ride to school.

These buggies don't just sit around. They're featured in the town's Fiesta Parade during the annual Old Spanish Days celebration each summer. The museum also exhibits more than fifty antique saddles, including some that seated some famous riders, including Ronald Reagan, Will Rogers, Clark Gable, and the Cisco Kid, as well as eight Visalia saddles made in 1866.

A virtual tour of the carriage museum is available at www.sbceo.k12.ca.us/~crane/carriage. The museum is located at 129 Castillo Street and can be reached by calling (805) 962–2353.

ONE VERY SHADY TREE

*I*n 1876 an Australian sailor visiting California was smit-
ten with a Santa Barbara girl. No one knows now
whether love blossomed between the two, but something truly
magnificent took root from that long-ago encounter. The
sailor presented the girl with the seedling of a Moreton Bay
fig tree, which she duly planted. One year later the tree was
moved to a spot downtown, and there the new arrival took
firmly to its new country. At present that seedling is a towering giant, the largest Moreton Bay fig tree in North America.

The tree spreads its massive roots in a grassy area near
the train depot. It stands 180 feet tall and has a branch
spread of almost 170 feet. Estimates—and it hasn't been
tried yet—are that 16,000 people could stand under its
shade. Dozens of tourists stop by daily to gawk and attempt
one of the hardest vacation pictures ever—capturing a person posing in front of the tree and getting its entire span in
the frame. Inevitably, the poser comes out looking like a dot
in the print.

The tree sprawls out at Chapala and Montecito Streets.
Santa Barbara designated it a landmark in 1976, meaning
that the city pledges to make sure this immigrant's roots are
firmly planted for generations to come.

A fig tree that had no problem spreading out.

C*HALK* T*HIS* O*NE* U*P* *FOR* C*HARITY*
S*anta* B*arbara*

K athy Koury, executive director of the Children's Creative
Project, proposed a most unusual idea for a fund-raiser for
the arts-education organization. Let's give a bunch of artists
some chalk, she said, and then let them mark up the grounds
of Santa Barbara's Old Mission. Koury had her reasons. She
had just returned from Italy, where she had experienced a
street-painting festival in the village of Grazie di Curtatone.
The festival is known as I Madonnari, and it's a centuries-old
tradition where artists roam from village to village and transform town squares into colorful and grand works of art.
Koury's idea was to bring this concept to America and present
it as a fund-raiser, with sponsors purchasing street-painting
squares.

The first U.S. chalk-painting festival was held in Santa Barbara's Mission in 1986, and now Santa Barbara's I Madonnari
street-painting festival is held each Memorial Day and attracts
thousands of visitors. The festival's success has spawned similar events at other American cities.

Several dozen artists paint sections of pavement of the Santa
Barbara Mission's plaza in a variety of colors, re-creating classic works of art or crafting remarkably detailed and vibrant
original works. Each year a featured artist is awarded a large
square and given several days to create the festival's central
work. Kids can also create with chalk on smaller squares,
which can be purchased during the festival.

This is art without any permanence. Now matter how beautiful or admired, no chalk drawing lasts more than a day.

For more information on Santa Barbara's I Madonnari festival, visit www.imadonnarifestival.com or call (805) 569–3873.

A MEATY TRADITION
Santa Maria

Barbecue isn't so much a meal option here as a way of life and a source of deep civic pride. It's a place where residents grow up knowing cuts of meat like the back of their hand and where barbecue is the only entrée option for gatherings of any size.

The Santa Maria Elks barbecue team in 1960. Photo: Santa Maria Valley Historical Society Museum.

Barbecue has to be done just right here, or there will be howls of protest, not to mention indigestion. Santa Maria-style barbecue began in the nineteenth century, when cattle ranches were all over the Central Coast. When they needed to feed large numbers of vaqueros and their families during roundups, they would carve out a large pit and grill meat skewered on tree limbs over a fire of red-oak coals. A Men's Club in the 1920s held monthly stag barbecues that carried on the barbecue tradition, and now every organization in town has its own barbecue pit. The only bone of contention here is whether to use top block sirloin or the triangular bottom sirloin, known as tri-tip. Loyalties for a cut of meat are fierce in this town.

The city has declared itself the barbecue capital of the world. Its identity is so well tied to its smoked meat that the Chamber of Commerce copyrighted the recipe for Santa Maria barbecue. It's nothing fancy: sirloin meat rolled in salt, pepper, and garlic salt and then put on steel rods and roasted over red-oak coals. It's served immediately when ready, accompanied by toasted French bread, local pinquito beans, and a tossed green salad. The only condiment is salsa, if you wish. Don't even think about sauce.

You don't have to look hard to find a barbecue in this town. Just take a walk around and follow your nose and the telltale clouds of smoke. If you're headed for a wedding here, one thing's for sure: You won't be getting chicken.

A STORE ON THE CUTTING EDGE
Solvang

If you stop by David Harvey's shop, he'll have a point or two to offer, in fact, hundreds, and they'll all be on the end of a blade. His Nordic Knives store is filled with sharp-edged

If it cuts, slices, or dices, David Harvey probably sells it.

devices of all kinds, including cooking knives, replica swords, cleavers, daggers, and battle axes. There are even slicing tools for tomatoes and trimmers for your nose and ear hair.

The real appeal here is not the mundane kitchen carver, however, but decorative, handcrafted knives much too dignified for humdrum duty such as slicing celery. These are art pieces, with jeweled handles that are just as beautiful as they are potentially deadly. Many of these items can cost a few thousand dollars.

Plenty of visitors are collectors, who drop by at least once a year for the town's annual Knife Show, produced by the store and featuring some of the top decorative knife makers in the country.

True to its name, the store carries a few Scandinavian knives. The shop's logo also pokes fun at the town's Danish decor, as it features a windmill with four different knives as its radiating vanes.

The store is located at 1634-C Copenhagen Drive and has a very sharp presence on the Internet at www.nordicknives.com.

THE GREAT DANES OF CALIFORNIA
Solvang

Folks from this Danish outpost like to boast that visiting Danes often remark how Solvang is more like Denmark than Denmark. True enough. You can't knock the authenticity of this town's attention to Danish culture, architecture, and cuisine, from its windmills and wood-carved doorways right down to its pastry and smorgasbord.

For good reason then Solvang is the self-proclaimed Danish capital of America. Danish immigrants from the Midwest settled the town in 1911 and opened a Danish folk school as its spiritual center. The school's gone now, but there are plenty of remnants of the town's Danish ancestry amid the tourist-minded shops and restaurants.

The town hosts an annual Danish Days celebration, an event that began in 1936 when the Danish king and queen paid a visit. For a genuine Danish experience, drop by the Elverhoy Museum, in a house built to resemble an eighteenth-century Danish farmhouse.

Solvang is a town proud of its Danish heritage.

Past the hand-carved door you'll be greeted by a costumed docent and led to several rooms documenting Danish culture and Solvang history. One display case features artifacts brought to this country by immigrating Danes, including old photos, coins, pipes, and clothing. There's a Danish farmhouse kitchen with hand-painted floral wall panels, pine countertops, and an antique stove with a traditional pan used to cook Aebelskiver, traditional round Danish pancakes.

The museum is at 1624 Elverhoy Way and can be reached by calling (805) 686–1211. You can visit the town on the Web at www.solvangusa.com.

HOG WILD FOR VINTAGE MOTORCYCLES
Solvang

Virgil Elings is a little coy about how many antique motorcycles he has. "If you know how many you have, you probably don't have too many," he observes. And Virgil has quite a few. Some are in his garage, of course. Others are all over his office and home, including his bedroom and dining room. "People come in and ask, 'Don't they mess up the rug?' I have to remind them that it's my rug," he says.

A 1936 Nimbus, one of many vintage bikes at the Solvang Motorcycle Museum. Photo: Mike Rogers, Greenhat Graphics.

Elings estimates he has about one hundred vintage racing motorcycles, easily making his fleet one of the most diverse private collections in the country. The oldest dates from 1904. Many are European, including a 1936 Danish Nimbus with sidecar and a 1926 British Sunbeam road bike.

Elings says that his love affair with motorcycles stems from his teenage years, when he rode one from Iowa to California and back. He also has raced for many years on the vintage racing circuit.

"My gut feeling is that it's a bank account you can enjoy," he says of his collection. He opened a motorcycle museum in 2000 in a former clothing store with maple floors, which turned out to be a good surface to handle oil leaks.

The museum is open on weekends during the afternoon and by appointment at other times. Call (805) 686–9522 for more information or motor over to the museum's Web site at www.motosolvang.com, where you can view the collection on-line.

On the Spirited Trail of Coastal Ghosts
Ventura

Richard Senate remembers his first ghost sighting in 1978. He was working on an archaeology project at a mission near Monterey when he came upon a man dressed in a monk's robe. As he walked over to talk with him, the monk vanished. "At first I thought he had fallen into a hole. Then I realized he had just disappeared right in front of my eyes," Senate recalls.

Senate has been stalking ghosts ever since. There isn't a ghost along the Central Coast that he hasn't heard about or perhaps even seen himself. He has written several books on haunting hot spots in California and leads popular ghost tours

IT REALLY WAS A JUNGLE OUT THERE

*T*he romance between Louis Goebel and Kathleen Parks *was hardly typical. They were neighbors in Thousand Oaks in the 1920s, when the town was mostly dusty roads, cattle ranches, and a few rural homesteads. She had cows; he had lions. His lions disturbed her cows, so she went over to complain. They married six months later.*

Together they ran one of Thousand Oaks' most beloved and noteworthy entertainments: a wild-animal amusement park known as Jungleland.

Louis Goebel brought six lions to Thousand Oaks in 1927 and opened up a lion farm. He married Kathleen a year later, and they acquired hundreds of wild animals, training some for movie roles, including MGM's famed Leo the lion. Jungleland lived up to its name, accommodating more than one hundred lions as well as giraffes, monkeys, gorillas, tigers, water buffalos, and elephants. Top animal trainers worked at Jungleland and put on quite a show. Jungleland thrilled visitors for four decades before it ran into financial troubles in the 1960s. Its closure in 1969 spawned one heck of a garage sale. More than 25,000 people attended the Jungleland auction and bid on everything from used circus wagons to more than 1,800 exotic animals.

At present the former Jungleland parcel presents more sophisticated fare, as it's the site of the city's performance-arts center, which offers music, dance, and theater.

Richard Senate believes that many ghosts haunt Ventura.
Photo: Debra Senate.

through Ventura, where he works as a city historian.

To tourists Ventura appears as a quaint California beach town. But to Senate and others, it's a ghoulish gulag, sheltering dozens of restless spirits wandering about historic sites and popular hangouts. At the city's Olivas Adobe, built in 1847, several people, including Senate, have seen a mysterious lady in black roaming about. A local Thai restaurant was plagued with so many ghostly appearances that the owner built an altar to keep the phantoms away. Visitors to the city's Bella Maggiore Inn may want to avoid room 17, where Senate says Lady Sylvia hanged herself and frequently returns in spirit form. "She likes to play tricks on people," Senate observes.

Senate has documented more than 600 ghost sightings in Ventura, leading him to call it one of the most haunted cities in the country. Senate offers ghost-walking tours, mostly in October, if you'd like to see for yourself. Call (805) 658–4726 for more information or visit Senate's Web site at www.ghost stalker.com.

VERY QUICK SAND
Ventura

Many folks head to the seaside to escape the hectic pace of life. The ocean's sounds and scents prompt many to plop down on a towel and just get quiet with one notable exception: the thrill seekers who rush to the Jim Hall Kart Racing School, America's longest-running kart-training facility and the only one boasting a paved beachside race course.

The object here is to roar around a half-mile track at speeds approaching 100 mph, careening around S-curves and hairpin swerves and a tortuous inner loop. The school's track has a gorgeous setting amid scenic coastal dunes with picturesque

A beautiful setting, if you can admire the scenery at 100 mph. Photo: Chris Jenson.

ocean views. But never mind that. Your helmeted noggin will be bobbing up and down so much you'll be challenged to focus on the postcard snapshots on the horizon. Just staying on course is the main goal. And forget about listening to soothing sounds of the ocean as your kart's engine drowns out any ambient noise.

Karts are miniature Indy cars used for training by aspiring professional race drivers. Recreational thrill seekers also take them for a few spins at the school, which provides training, karts, and required safety gear. One thing's clear: These aren't dune buggies, dude, so buckle up. For information take a spin over to www.jhrkartracing.com or speed-dial (805) 654–1329.

S *weet* C *reams*
Ventura

Most people's understanding of chocolate is very limited, as in "Chocolate, mmmm, tastes good." But chocolate is a complex treat with a history and science as rich as mousse. The Aztecs believed, for example, that chocolate held the key to gaining knowledge and power. More recently, studies have shown that chocolate eaters tend to live longer than those who don't indulge. Countless suitors approaching their prey with a box of chocolates will attest to cocoa's potency as an aphrodisiac.

Now innovative spas are enriching chocolate's scope of benevolence with an array of new body treatments that feature chocolate creams and lotions. Ahead of the curve is the Spa by Diane Loring at Ventura's historic Pierpont Inn. The spa offers several cocoa-themed and truly decadent treatments including a chocolate contour body wrap. You can get smeared in a chocolate skin treatment that not only smells heavenly but also detoxifies. Loring says that it's "quite lovely, like chocolate fondue." Then there's the chocolate mineral buff. While sea salt exfoliates the skin, senses are tantalized with whiffs of cocoa in a special coating. You become something of a human dessert as the buff is finalized with an application of chocolate-whipped-cream body lotion.

"It's totally nonfattening and fun," Loring says, "with excellent results in smoothing, firming, and contouring your body." Alas, the same cannot be said of a luscious bonbon.

The spa is one sweet call away at (805) 477–1847.

SEARCHING FOR EVIDENCE OF A MYSTERY WRITER'S ROOTS
Ventura

E rle Stanley Gardner began a stellar law career in Ventura in 1915, specializing in defending courtroom underdogs and helping to free prisoners unjustly convicted. He was also an amateur archaeologist, hunter, wildlife photographer, and rancher. Somehow he also found time to become one of America's most prolific authors, writing more than 155 books and 400 articles.

Even with these impressive credentials, Gardner's fame is overshadowed by his most famous creation: Perry Mason, the fictional and beloved defense lawyer. Gardner published his first Perry Mason novel, *The Case of the Velvet Claws,* while practicing law in Ventura in 1933. Many of the characters and settings for the Perry Mason series were based on Gardner's experiences here. The courtroom set for the Perry Mason television show starring Raymond Burr was modeled on the real one in Ventura, where Gardner had argued many of his most important cases.

Some locals in Ventura consider it a mystery as to why more hasn't been done to mark Gardner's literary roots in Ventura. There's a small plaque on Gardner's old office building and an occasional walking tour of some Gardner haunts. Locals John Anthony Miller and Keith Burns believe a permanent museum in the downtown area is what's really needed. They've collected a bunch of Gardner memorabilia, including his old typewriter, law books, and even his baby cup, as well as copies of his books

John Anthony Miller with some of the artifacts from the
Erle Stanley Gardner Museum. Photo: Courtesy of Erle
Stanley Gardner Museum.

and old scripts and props from the television series. At the
moment they display these items in a bookmobile on a temporary basis, carting it to occasional events.

At the very least, they're suggesting that an alleyway near
Gardner's old office be changed. The new name? Della Street.

You can see the Erle Stanley Gardner virtual museum by
clicking on www.erlestanleygardner.com.

Index

Avocado Festival, 105–6
Badwater UltraMarathon
   185–86
Baker, 179–81
Baker, Bob, 26–28
Bakersfield, 181, 183
Bart's Books, 226–28
Baseball Reliquary, 67–69
Beal, Art, 220–21
Becket, Marta, 186–87
Bell, Claude, 140–41
Big Dog Parade, 244–46
Blessing of the Animals,
   31–32
Blessing of the Cars, 85
Boron, 183, 185
Borrego Springs, 139–40
Bubble Gum Alley, 241
Buena Park, 93–94
Bunny Museum, The, 71–73
Burbank, 55–56
Cabazon, 140–41
Calabasas, 56–57
California Strawberry
   Festival 231–33
Camarillo, 219–20
Cambria, 220–21
Carlsbad, 94–97
Carriage and Western Art
   Museum, 246–47
Carrot Festival, 145
Cholla Cactus Garden, 153
Clam Festival, 236
Coronado, 97–99

Crespo, Clare, 41, 43
Crystal Cathedral, 108–9
Culver City, 1–4
Dana Point, 99–101
Death Valley 185–86
Death Valley Junction,
   186–87
Death Valley National Park,
   187–90, 192, 194–98
Del Mar, 101–2
Desert Christ Park, 174–75
Doo Dah Parade, 79
Dresden Room, 47–48
Duck-a-thon, 110
Early Man Site, 216–17
Earp, Wyatt, 132–34
East Los Angeles, 4–5
Echo Park, 6–7
Edwards Air Force Base,
   198–99
Ehn, John, 90–91
Elings, Virgil, 255–56
El Pedorrero Muffler
   Shop, 4–5
Elverhoy Museum, 253–54
Encounter Lounge, 24, 26
Escondido, 102, 105
Exotic Feline Breeding
   Compound, 208–09
Exotic World Burlesque
   Museum, 200–201
Fallbrook, 105–08
Farmer John Murals, 89–90
Faulkner, Eve 125–26

Felicity, 142–43
Flower Fields, 96–97
Forestiere, Baldasare,
    199, 202
Freiberg, Gary, 238–39
Fresno, 199, 202
Frymer, Jeff, 39–41
Garden Grove, 108–9
Gardner, Erle Stanley,
    262–63
George C. Page Museum, 28,
    30–31
Golf Cart Parade, 157–58
Gubler Orchids, 150–52
Hatch, Bob, 73, 76
Haute Dog Easter Parade,
    The, 57–59
Hemet, 143–45
Hollywood, 8–15
Hollywood Entertainment
    Museum, 10–12
Hollywood Forever
    Cemetery, 8–10
Holtville, 145
Holyland Exhibition, 43–45
Hotel Del Coronado, 97–99
Howard, Bob, 99–101
101 Cafe, 123–25
Huntington Beach, 110–15
Huntington Botanical
    Gardens, 86
I Madonnari, 249
Imperial Beach, 115–16
Indio, 146–49
Inglewood, 15–16
Integraton, 152, 154
International Surfing
    Museum, 113–15
Irrelevant Week, 121–23

Isla Vista Jugglers
    Convention, 244
Istel, Jacques, 142–43
Jessop's Clock, 131–32
Jim Hall Kart Racing
    School, 259–60
Johnstone, Al and Janet,
    136–37
Julian, 149–50
Kelso Dunes, 205–6
Kester, Ernie "Doc," 168
Kingsburg, 202–3
Kirsner, Mel, 149–50
Knight, Leonard, 156
La Jolla, 119–21
Laguna Beach, 118
Landers, 150–52, 154,
Laurel Canyon, 17–18
Lawrence Welk Museum,
    102, 105
LEGOLAND, 94–96
London, Bill, 4–5
Lone Pine, 203
Long Beach, 57–66
Los Angeles, Greater, 55–91
Los Angeles, Metropolitan,
    1–53
Los Angeles Pet Memorial
    Park, 56–57
Los Angeles River, 33–35
Los Feliz, 35–36
Lotusland, 222
Lynwood, 66–67
McPherson, Aimee
    Semple, 6–7
Madonna Inn, 242
Marina del Rey, 36–37
Marionette Theater, 26–28
Martin, Antone, 174–75

Mitchell Caverns, 207–8
Mojave National Preserve, 205–6
Monrovia, 67–69
Montecito, 222
Montz, Larry, 36–37
Morro Bay, 224–26
Movieland Ranch, 173–74
Movieland Wax Museum, 93–94
Museum of Death, 32–33
Museum of Jurassic Technology, 3–4
Museum of Neon Art, 22–24
National Date Festival, 146–47
Newport Beach, 121–23
Niland, 156
Nit Wit Ridge, 220–21
Nordic Knives, 251–53
Northridge, 69, 71
Oceanside, 123–25
Ojai, 226–31
Orange, 125–26
Oxnard, 231–33
Pageant of the Masters, 118
Palm Desert, 157–58
Palm Springs, 158–65
Palm Springs Follies, 158, 161
Park Bench Cafe, 111–13
Parkfield, 206–07
Pasadena, 71–76, 78–79
Pioneertown, 165–66, 168
Pismo Beach, 233, 236–38
Prisbrey, Tressa, 84
Providence Mountains, 207–08
Queen Mary, 64–66

Raisin Festival, 211
Ramona, 126–28
Ramona Pageant, 143–45
Randy's Donuts, 15–16
Richardson, Noble, 170–71
Riegler, Gil, 126–28
Rodia, Simon, 49–50
Rolling Hills, 81
Rosamond, 208–9
San Diego, 128–37
San Luis Obispo, 238–42
Santa Barbara, 244–49
Santa Maria, 250–51
Santa Monica, 37–41
Schmitt, Anthony, 37, 39
Schofield, Grant, 181–83
Scott, Walter, 194–95
Scotty's Castle, 194–95
Searles Valley, 209–10
Selma, 211
Senate, Richard, 256–59
Sheehy, Patrick, 1–3
Shepard, Jesse, 128–29
Shields, Floyd, 147–48
Shonholtz, Sig, 52–53
Sierra Madre, 82–83
Silent Movie Theatre, The, 12, 14–15
Silver Lake, 41–48
Simi Valley, 84
Skeletons in the Closet, 21–22
Skinny House, 59–61
Smith, Thomas "Pegleg", 139–40
Solvang, 251–56
Solvang Motorcycle Museum, 255–56
Stuart, George, 228, 230
Studio City, 48–49

Sylmar, 85

Teakettle Junction, 189–90

Tehachapi, 214

Thomas, David, 225–26

Trona Pinnacles, 209–10

Twentynine Palms, 170–73

U.S. Open Sandcastle
    Competition, 115–16

Ubehebe Crater, 187–89

Van Nuys, 88

Van Tassel, George, 152, 154

Ventura, 256, 259–63

Vernon, 89–90

Villa Montezuma, 128–29

Vinyl Record Day, 238–39

Walska, Ganna, Madame, 222

Watts Towers, 49–50

Watts, 49–50

Welburn, Doug, 106–7

West Hollywood 52–53

Westchester, 50–52

Western Foundation of
    Vertebrate Zoology,
    219–10

Winchester, 173–74

Wisteria Festival, 82–83

Woodland Hills, 90–91

Yermo, 216–17

Yucca Valley, 174–75

About the Author

S aul Rubin is a veteran California journalist who has covered everything from major disasters to stories highlighting the state's quirky inhabitants and culture. He has written for the *Los Angeles Times* and Copley News Service and was also a staff writer for a national sports magazine show on Fox Sports Net.

In addition to writing books and the occasional freelance article, Saul teaches journalism at Santa Monica College and lives in the Los Angeles area. Whatever he does to make a living, Saul knows that his real job is keeping his wife and daughter happy.